FIRE YOUR JOB

How To Become Your Own Boss & Find Financial Independence

Akilan Aks Theva
Award Winning Author

10-10-10
Publishing

Fire Your Job
www.fireyourjobbook.com
Copyright © 2018 Akilan Aks Theva

ISBN: 978-1-77277-201-2

Limits of Liability and Disclaimer of Warranty
The author and publisher shall not be liable for your misuse of the enclosed material. This book is strictly for informational and educational purposes only.

Warning – Disclaimer
The purpose of this book is to educate and entertain. The author and/or publisher do not guarantee that anyone following these techniques, suggestions, tips, ideas, or strategies will become successful. The author and/or publisher shall have neither liability nor responsibility to anyone with respect to any loss or damage caused, or alleged to be caused, directly or indirectly by the information contained in this book.

Medical Disclaimer
The medical or health information in this book is provided as an information resource only, and is not to be used or relied on for any diagnostic or treatment purposes. This information is not intended to be patient education, does not create any patient-physician relationship, and should not be used as a substitute for professional diagnosis and treatment.

Publisher
10-10-10 Publishing
Markham, ON
Canada

Printed in Canada and the United States of America

Table of Contents

Dedication

I am dedicating this book to my loving affectionately cared late father Thevathurai Rasiah for raising me as a confident man and supportive of my decisions.

Acknowledgements

I am so grateful to have my family and friends who are very supportive of me all the time. I am thankful to my caring, affectionate mom, and my late father, whom I admire for helping people without any expectation in return. I am so grateful to my brothers, Jay and Shan, who trusted me and invested with me in my initial real estate investment projects, even though I was green as grass in investing in real estate at that time. I am lucky to have an ever welcoming and caring sister and sisters-in-law.

My special thanks to my wife, Tharshy, for standing beside me on new, transformational changes in my career, and for taking care of me and the kids, with unconditional love. It is a remarkable journey we have embarked on. Thank you to my children, Akshay and Ashika, for letting my mind refresh all the time, and for motivating me with your thoughts. Ashika, I would like to recognize you for changing my book title, at the age of 9, from Fire Your Boss to Fire Your Job.

I am very much honored to do business with my investment partners, in Ottawa and Toronto, who trusted me with their hard-earned money. I am very pleased that I was able to offer my real estate investment advice, and be part of the executive team of Skyvision Group INC. I wish you good luck in the coming years to reach multi million dollars in investment.

As I write this, the team of engineers at one of my companies, BisRing (bisring.com), are working hard for the success of the company. I am blessed to have my dedicated team who are spending their valuable family time on my passionate idea, turned into a technology company, which will be a great success in the coming years.

I would like to appreciate Hans Molin and Darrell Wellington, at Syntronic Canada's executive team, for being supportive of my decision to Fire My Job after a successful engineering project, and still be good friends with me.

I would like to thank Victor Menace for introducing me to Raymond Aaron, and George Ross, Mr. Trump's former executive vice president. My first real estate investing book that I read was written by Mr. George Ross—thank you for writing that great book, Trump Strategies for Real Estate. I would like to thank Selva Vettyvel, CEO of Home Life Future, for acknowledging my expertise and for advising me to take real estate investment to the next level.

Thank you, Raymond Aaron, for teaching me the importance of branding, and the step by step process of writing a book. I would like to thank Cara Witvoet for motivating and supporting me to get this book done. Finally, I am so grateful to God for giving me the strength to think positively in any situation, and come out of it better than before.

Foreword

Do you dream of becoming financially independent? To do so requires a lot of discipline, courage and dedication, and if you don't have a plan, you can find yourself buried within your busy schedule. In Fire Your Job, Akilan Aks Theva outlines the steps he has taken in his own life, overcoming obstacles and failures, to reach success.

Some of the lessons covered are:

* time is limited, and you should not get too comfortable in your current life

* how to turn all your negative frustration into positive energy that can be a catalyst to your success

* you don't need million dollar properties to get the required monthly passive income to become financially independent and pursue your dream

Fire Your Job will help you reach success by fine-tuning your attitude, thinking process, and analyzing skills, and learning how to associate with the right people. You don't need a lot of money or education to be an entrepreneur. Being successful has to be defined by you, and you must be determined to achieve your goals.

If you aspire to be successful in your career, or you want to become financially independent and do what you enjoy, this is the book for you.

Raymond Aaron
New York Times Bestselling Author

Chapter 1

Introduction

Dream to Become Independent

Every day, waking up in the morning, going to work, and looking forward to the breaks, and then getting excited about Friday, is what ninety-nine percent of us are accustomed to. It kind of gives us a secure and comfortable life, like trained cattle, but is our inner mind happy about what is happening day-to-day in our life? This is something we should be able to answer ourselves. What motivates us every day to get up and go to work? For many people, monthly bills and food on the table motivates them to go to work; otherwise, they would be left without shelter and food. If they had an alternative option, how many of them would continue to go to work? We will learn this in the coming chapters.

I enjoy talking to people and sharing good thoughts. One day, I was attending a seminar and had to grab a sandwich during the lunch break. I was planning to have a quick one, and take care of some of my business executions over the phone. After I ordered my sandwich, and finished my phone calls, I started to talk to the cashier. She was the only one there, and it was around 1:30 pm. She seemed to be very active and tried to sell me more than what I intended to buy. After seeing her enthusiasm, and out of curiosity, I asked her if she was the owner of the business. She said, "No, my boss owns it, and he went on a vacation. I am just an employee, working for him for many years, and running his business". I realized, working at a coffee shop for many years, and being there like a manager, she must be making roughly $2500 per month. Just to get to know what was running through her mind, I asked her another question. If I said you have another way of earning $3000 per month, not working for someone, would you still be doing this job? Her answer was, "Hmmmm, what would I do at home? It would be boring." She had not thought about the billions of amazing things she could do with her life; instead, she thinks like 99% of the people. In her mind, she was thinking about sitting at her home, eating, and watching TV. Definitely, she should not do that, and she was not thinking about being out of her comfortable little routine she has.

I recall many people saying the same thing: "No, I cannot sit at home." They would say, "I enjoy going to work and talking to people, more than sitting at home." Wow, what are you going to talk about at work? Corporate politics? Gossip about the colleagues, or complain about the life, weather, and news? Does any of this matter to you, or your family, or your community you are living in? Definitely, no! Have you thought about spending more time with your loved ones, and making changes in the community and in the world? Nobody has to sit at home and twiddle their thumbs. The universe is filled with tremendous opportunities and endless growth. Whatever desire you have, eventually you will achieve. There is no harm in desiring something great and big.

Being Independent and Determined

Being independent teaches people how to do things on their own, and will make them learn the details of the subject matter they are dealing with. It would be a very strong habit to develop from the beginning. When you know more about a subject, or business deal during the negotiation, you are in a better position than your counterpart. When you work with partners on a project, you would be in a position to bring something valuable to the table. People respect a person who has a wealth of knowledge. No matter what hurdles you may encounter, you have to make sure your target is achieved. If you are a student, and want to complete your diploma or degree, just put yourself into it and get it done. I have a very good example: when I was in university, I hated the course, Introduction to Computer Electronics. Once a week, around 2 pm, the lecture would start after lunch time. It would last for three hours. It was taught by an elderly lecturer who had no humor. I had a habit of not missing any lectures, no matter how late I had been up the night before. Being that I had just had lunch, and he was a boring lecturer, I would barely be able to keep my eyes open to listen to him.

The midterm marks came out, and I got an A+ for physics, and got a D (In Canada, D is 50–55%, so I almost failed.) for this subject. I enjoy applied math and visualization. This course required a lot of memorizing, but I lacked, big time, in memorizing things. He was teaching about the first computer, where people go inside the computer and work on it. These days, we are accustomed to carrying a computer, called a smart phone, in our palm. Since I got a D, I decided to drop the course and take it in the next semester. Just before dropping the course,

3

I went and saw the professor to get his advice. I told him, due to having very low marks, I was planning to drop the course. He looked into my eyes, and asked me, "Are you stupid? What are you here for? If you are here to study and pass the course, you had better be focused and serious, and then you will pass the subject." I told myself that I would be determined; and I took it very seriously, abandoned my idea of dropping the course, and continued. With my hard work, even though I did not enjoy it, I got the required passing mark at the end of the semester. Being determined is a very important, interpersonal skill to be successful. If you are not confident, and you deter your focus numerous times, you will have less chance of being successful.

If you are analyzing a business deal, and you are the sole owner or the executer, make sure to get advice from someone in the relevant field. In 2008, I was analyzing a property to acquire in Toronto, but everyone, including my realtor, wasn't happy that I bought that property. Everyone I was close to hated it, including my wife, but I was determined to purchase for various reasons. I was visualizing, at the time, how creatively I was going to increase the cash flow and the future potential, and how I could force the appreciation. Today, that is my best investment I ever made so far. From a single property, I am getting $2300 net positive cash flow. Another great thing is that I own the property for free now. If you want to know more details, check the bonus section at **www.fireyourjobbook.com**. I don't lift a leaf at the property, because I have a team to take care of the property management. If I would have neglected the idea, because others advised me, I would have regretted it big time. What would they advise me now??? If you want to be in the top one percent, you better know what you are doing, and stand by your decision.

Real estate investment is not like eating a piece of cake. It involves discipline and courage to handle all sorts of issues. If the tenants don't pay the rent, you have to negotiate with them to make them pay the rent, or legally evict them out of your place. Especially in Canada, the law is tenant-sided, and bad apples may misuse this. I had numerous experiences with all sort of scenarios. My advice would be to follow the list of items below, to be successful in real estate investment.

1) Try to buy a property at a discounted price, as much as possible.
2) Make sure the area where the property is located has high potential for future appreciation.
3) Visualize how you could force the appreciation.
4) Be creative enough to increase the cash flow.
5) Learn by doing it, and get yourself educated.
6) Treat each property like a separate small business.
7) Make sure you have access to liquid cash, for at least 6-months' worth of expenses.
8) Maintain professionalism during tenant handling.
9) Even if the tenant offered to take on responsibilities, do not let it go if that was not part of the initial lease agreement. It may bite you big time, later.
10) Always document every major issue.
11) Keep all the financial receipts, for each property, in a separate envelope. Your accountant will like you.
12) Never be cheap. Make sure to spend money on all the necessary maintenance, and if an experienced, expensive lawyer needs to be hired, never hesitate.
13) Prepare to be dynamic enough to change your strategies.
14) Don't be shy to hold hands with an expert rather than running away from it.

15) Continuous education and self-motivation is critically important.
16) Form a team of experts (Virtual Team) in the locations where you have investment properties.

One of my colleagues would tell me his horror story of a bad tenant he had, who did not want to pay him the rent for a few months. Eventually, the tenant left the property, and left it badly damaged. He had to spend thousands to bring that back to a normal condition, and then sold it. He told me that he would never, ever own an investment property. It was unfortunate that he had a bad tenant, but he wasn't determined enough. Even though I went through a much higher scale of horror experience, I was highly determined, and took every issue as a learning experience.

Thinking Big and Long-Term Vision

Whether you are working at a factory, a restaurant, or a big corporation, don't just focus on your day-to-day activities, and bury yourself. Most people talk about the news, go on social network, or watch YouTube videos during the work break times. All of these activities are not going to elevate us from being the broke and middle class ninety-nine percent of people. For an example, if you are working at a coffee shop as a coffee server, like Tim Horton's, you would only require minimum education. If you start to work there, you should not think, "Oh, I am working for minimum wage and running around like a headless chicken, every day, and it is not taking me anywhere." If I were you, I would be good in what I do, and try to learn all the ground level activities taking place at the coffee shop. Show you are capable of doing more than just serving the coffee. Once you learn the process, now think about owning one. These days, Tim Horton's requires an owner to be part of the operation team. They want a committed owner to run the business, and not a passive investor, potentiallly may damage their reputation, not knowing the culture, and just focussing on the profit of the single store. There are many people with money who wanted to run that business, but they don't have the time to put themselves at the coffee shop to serve the customers. Now, your expertise becomes a highly preferred asset to the investors. Once you have accumulated enough knowledge, and have talked to the investors, surely you have a very good chance to run the business with an investment partner. If you are one of them in the Greater Toronto Area, feel free to contact me by going to **www.fireyourjobbook.com**. We may have a great business opportunity. Only by thinking big, you could go to the next level. If you aim very high, you may even be able to achieve something somewhere in the middle ground. If you don't aim for anything, you achieve nothing.

Another example is, if you have work experience from an investment bank, you could create your own investment company that could be funded via family and friends. As long as you don't practise what you do at work, and disclose your experimental business to your human resource or legal department, you won't get into a conflict of interest. While I was a full time employee in the high tech industry, I started my real estate investment and a property management company. I never had any conflict of interest or let down the projects I was working on. Sometimes I was even working on the weekends, and late evenings, because the project had to be finished as per the dead line. Some employees would work hard for the bonus of 4%, 8%, or 12%. In my case, I invested in a property in Toronto, sold it within one year, and got $30 000 as net gain. If you make $100 000 per year, that would be 30% bonus. That is absolutely great, and the wealth of knowledge you will acquire is going to multiply in your future projects. Would you rather work overtime and ask for a bonus from your manager, who won't be able to disperse, or would you rather have your own experimental business, and get your own great bonuses? If you think deeply, you have a higher chance of becoming an entrepreneur, either in your field of expertise or in something new. In any adventures, long-term vision is highly critical.

I was so hesitant to buy my first property as my primary residence; I had a student loan and a few credit card debts. Since I am the first immigrant to Canada, there was no support from my parents, or inherited wealth to pay my tuitions. Having a student loan and a credit card loan were the only way, at the time, to get through four years of university. The traditional way, of the parents' advice, is to not accumulate loans. Having a loan is taboo. What I did was pay off my student loan within two years, with my lay-off bonus. What? Lay-off bonus? Sure; I will discuss this in later chapters. After the loan got paid off, I saved 20% down for a $250 000 house; and the closing cost and appliance purchase expense was another $10 000. I bought my first property in 2003, instead of buying it in the late nineties. It was one of the biggest mistakes I ever made. I could have bought my first property in the year 2000, and it would have appreciated well, and I wouldn't have lost thousands of dollars in the stock market. The time I started my career and my investment, was the dot com crash, and then the 9/11 issue. Wow, great timing for a newbie who did not have anyone to guide him either. I went through a horrible personal experience, and managed to get through it successfully.

Do Not Let the Negative Energy Take Over You

In our lives, we are dealing with various types of people. Most of the people only look at the negative side of anything. They only think of the glass half empty, while the successful people think of the glass half full—the rest can be easily filled, with little effort. Even though we don't want people to die or get hurt, that type of news always makes the headlines. If someone advises you in a negative way, don't waste your energy arguing with them. These kinds of situations won't be productive. Politely listen to them, and spend only a few minutes to analyze them. If anything tangible matters to you, you could make some changes in your decision. Almost all the time, you should be able to just ignore them. People don't realize, when they give negative comments to someone, they are unintentionally discouraging the motivated person. It also undermines someone's full potential, and jeopardizes their ambitions. Keeping your distance from negative commenters, and turning your TV off when there is discouraging news, would at least preserve your positive energy.

These days, social media has become a part of everyone's everyday life. If people use it to share their happy family moments, marketing activities, or business progress, that is great. Instead, some people use it for negative comments, and have gossip subgroups. As long as you are prepared to weed out the unnecessary garbage, and grab the matters important to you, it will lead you to great success and a happy life. Mind is everything. A person who has had a stroke may have a portion, or all, of his/her body become dysfunctional. This is not because their body part became defective; it is because the control signal from the brain is not reaching the body part to make the intended move. If our brain gets tired of negativity, and we don't feel the excitement about new adventures, then we stop producing great results for us, our family, our community, and the country we live in. When you are highly motivated and energized, nothing would stop you from achieving your target.

Keeping your energy high is highly critical as well. Having morning exercise or regular evening exercise, with a healthy diet, would be great. Some people make a New Year's resolution, such as going to the gym regularly, and changing their diet to one of a healthy lifestyle. They get the gym membership and buy the necessary gear. They visit the gym for the first few weeks in January, and then something comes up, and they miss a few days. It will turn into weeks, and then months, and then they don't have the courage to go back. Next year is already around the corner, and they get into another New Year's resolution. Excuses are for unsuccessful people. I am positive it will make you prepare yourself to be successful in any endeavours you are planning to achieve. I am excited that you will learn lot in the upcoming chapters...

Chapter 2

Being Disciplined and Dedicated

Nothing Happens Overnight

Fire Your Job strategy requires dedication and extra hard work to bring you to a comfortable and confident state. If you want to own a small business, you need to start accumulating knowledge about the industry you want to get in, or start doing it. Without any of these, the idea always stays in your brain and dies out. Many people, at least once in their life, would have thought about a business idea, but how many of them took the necessary steps to flourish their idea? If you have an idea about an adventurous project, which can be executed alone or needs partners, start writing up your business plan. Once you have the business plan, do the preliminary studies of how this business serves your customers. If you don't learn the idea that will be well received by the customers and benefitted by them, seldom will it be successful.

Once you have the business plan, and understand the potential in the market place, you can now start executing the necessary steps to the next level. If your weekends and nights have to be sacrificed during your feasibility study, so be it. There can be multiple business ideas that can be killed during the feasibility study, rather than discussing it with others, or starting the business and then realizing it has no future. Knowing what you are going to pitch to the potential investors is crucial. Most of the investors grow their wealth by being savvy. Savvy investors will torque with a lot of valuable questions that may even educate you.

When I thought to acquire my first investment property, I did area studies and chose a high end, upcoming neighborhood in the Greater Toronto Area. I was looking for potential investment properties for a year. Since, in 2008, the real estate meltdown started, and the banking system crashed around the world, I was expecting something major to happen in Canadian real estate markets as well. I saw the price decline by 10 to 15 percent in certain suburbs in the Greater Toronto Area, while the area in which I was focusing to buy stood up and did not experience any sign of a correction. Once I told my investment partner, who is one of my brothers, that I was putting in an offer and getting serious about it, he told me that he had good faith in my decision, and that he could be a passive investor and not participate in any of the active roles.

During this time, I was living in Ottawa, which is around 400 km away from Toronto. I was visiting almost every other week to look for properties and place offers. Once the property was acquired, I would travel Friday evenings to show the property to prospective tenants. I had listed on local realtor web sites to rent, using my real estate agent, but I managed to rent it for higher rent, and much faster, with my creative idea. I could have hired someone to take care of marketing, screening the prospects, and tenant handling, but the lesson I have learned by doing it was tremendous. This allowed me to form a property management and acquisition teams in Toronto. This enabled me to manage day-to-day activities, and acquire more properties while I was living 400 km away from my investment properties. In small business ventures, I am a firm believer in doing the necessary research; and, step-by-step, getting things done would allow you to form the right team or hire the necessary services. If you are a person who does not want to get your hands dirty, it is better to associate or partner with credible people who have the courage and wealth of knowledge. As long as you are willing to give a certain percentage of the profit to the active partner, you could execute as many projects as per your capability.

Too Much Analysis Makes You Paralyzed

In decision making, or starting a business adventure, if you analyze too much, you get paralyzed. In any business start-up, probability of failure is high. If you are a first immigrant, or are from a non-wealthy family, you may not have someone to rely on for teaching you their secret source of their success. It is like ancient people touching the fire: they would have learned that it will burn. It is a similar philosophy: you have to try numerous adventures to identify what works for you. You could analyze to minimize the loss, but you cannot try to prevent any future failures one hundred percent. Facing failures are good hands-on and personalized lessons that cannot be learned at school or by attending seminars.

I was working at Blackberry at the time, and I was a prime designer for a radio technology called CDMA, on one of the versions of mobile Blackberry devices. After a best circuit optimization, everything was fine as a bare circuit board, but as soon as a device got assembled, using my circuit with a circuit-protecting metal Can on, almost half of the power is lost. Since almost all of us these days are using mobile devices, it could be an interesting discussion for you as well. For your knowledge, a radio frequency (RF) signal is like water—if there is a hole, it will get radiated or received, and the circuit that gets exposed would act like an antenna. Most of the radio frequency circuits and components get shielded to prevent any non-wanted signals from getting through and degrading the wanted signal. This particular situation became a challenge for me; and after numerous ideas, I came to a conclusion that the signal inside the shielded metal Can, on top of my circuit, was reflecting the signal inside and getting convoluted. Due to phase mismatch, it was cancelling some of the radio power. My manager asked me to go back and investigate by checking the circuit to see if I could fix it from the circuit optimization.

For your knowledge, radio frequency components don't work the way we simulate and design. It has to be optimized in the lab to get the best performance. I spent extra-long hours to identify exactly where the internal radiation and reflection was impacting the performance. During my experiments I made a small circular hole on the shielded Can to get rid of the material that was reflecting the signal. Wow, after assembling the device using the previously optimized circuit, and a hole in the shielded cover, the device was performing as designed. When I proposed the mechanical design change to my management team, they were puzzled initially. After all the necessary tests were conducted, it became the solution, and the management was happy. Blackberry sold a couple million devices with that change that I proposed; however, nobody thought about or appreciated it at the beginning. If I would have just followed the instructions given to me, I would not have provided a winning solution. If I would have sat down in front of the computer and simulated various scenarios, it would not have taken me anywhere. Thinking out of the box, and limiting your continuous analysis, will get you a winning solution.

Analyze Before Decision Making, and Stick With It

When partnering with someone, or starting new ventures, we should do proper preliminary screening to eliminate any bad partnerships or projects. Many people start out with friends and family, without any exit strategy or knowing who does what. They may have an idea about the sweet part of the project and how they are going to make lots of money, but many fail to dig deeper and analyse all the hidden costs and the manpower needed to pull it off as a successful venture. Every project should have an exit strategy that won't hinder anyone's reputation. If you start a partnership project without proper due diligence, you could let down the other partners due to lack of commitment. This particular incident may prevent you from getting into future partnership projects, even though you honestly wanted to make it happen. The previous experience you had with your partners would have already labelled you as a person who is not reliable.

I was once carpooling, from Toronto to Ottawa, with a software engineer friend of mine. On our way back, we were discussing multiple things. By the middle of our journey, we had an idea hatched about an online sales business for a particular product, which would serve busy parents and elderly people. The rest of the journey was all about that idea. We were so excited and, when we left the car, we set up a time after work to meet at my home office to discuss it further. We had a few consecutive meetings to discuss the name of the company, how to develop the web site, the hosting company, getting the seed financing, and so on. I told my friend to let me document all our discussions, our responsibilities, the required commitment from both of us, additional man power, and projected business growth, etc. We met again, and went through the details and how much commitment we would require every week to make it happen. Fortunately, my friend told me his honest opinion: "Wow, this requires lots of time, and needs the sacrifice of family time after work, and cannot be committed." Thankfully, we ended that idea on good terms, without anyone involving. If we had gotten seed money, and discussed the idea with more potential partners but bailed out in the middle of the project, or the project flopped due to lack of commitment, it would have damaged both of our reputations.

Be Dedicated and Disciplined

It is always great to explore any ideas, as long as they are meaningful. I have a philosophical thought about not leaving any doors unopened. You never know which one has the treasure behind it. If you start a project after the proper due diligence is done, you have to make sure the commitment is there, right till the end. As mentioned before, you cannot prevent any unexpected hurdles on the way to success, but if you are committed, you better find ways to resolve them, and march towards the success.

No matter what business or job you are in, if you are dedicated and act with credibility, the success is inevitable. Being dedicated, and delivering what you have promised, allows you to accumulate your positive credibility among your relatives, friends, neighbours, colleagues, and supervisors. It also creates a path for career growth, and invites potential business partners. When I was working at the start-up companies, or bigger companies, I made sure the product delivery was not impacted negatively due to my lack of commitment. I would make sure, within my area of control, that things were achieved without any delays. Whenever I lost a high paying job, I never had an issue finding another job. My last record-breaking example of finding another job after my private consulting ended, was getting a job the next day at Syntronic, with a promoted position. My previous manager was a director there, and he knew my expertise and the sincerity I had shown in the past at Blackberry.

Without long-term discipline, nothing tangible can be achieved. One incident may jeopardize years' worth of sacrifices. Being disciplined is critical to future success. If you slack at work, complain about not getting promoted, and cannot find a better paying job, it would be because of your poor interpersonal skills, more than anything else. When you do things with your heart in it, your productivity goes higher, and out-of-the box thinking grows as well. Being dedicated and disciplined requires lot of sacrifices. If you are a person who enjoys short-term happiness and lack of dedication, it is time to rethink and change your habits. This interpersonal skill is highly appreciated by the society, the work place, and the business partners. All of our actions are watched by everyone. We may think no one is noticing us, but our reputation is so much important to our success. I will walk you through how our reputation would impact our success in any aspect of our life.

Chapter 3

Reputation Requires Sacrifices

Do Not Damage Your Reputation and Then Try to Correct It

It may take a very long time to build your good reputation, and may need your entire life to sustain it. Keeping up a good reputation of whatever you do is very important. At home, parents like the good kids; at school, teachers appreciate the well-behaved and intelligent kids, who are on top of their homework. At work, managers and colleagues respect the people who are dependable, have expertise, can be relied on, and co-operate with others. Among friends, people would tend to get closer with a person whom they could trust—one who genuinely cares about them—and could socialize together comfortably.

When I was a kid, I read a story, which I would like to share with you. There was this little boy who was very naughty, and he had a very bad reputation at school and in the neighbourhood as well. The dad was advising the kid that being naughty and not respected by others is not good while growing up. He told the little boy that he was going to place a nail in the wall whenever he got complaints about the kid. Within a few weeks, the wall was filled with hundreds of nails. The boy was devastated to see so many nails in the wall that represented the number of complaints his dad had received. The day came when, finally, the boy told himself, from now on, he would be doing good things, and would impress his dad with good compliments from others. When the little boy shared this with his dad, they agreed that he could remove the nails from the wall for each positive compliment.

The days passed, and the little boy changed his bad behaviours into the best ones possible in order to get positive compliments, and remove the nails, one by one. Finally, he had managed to pull out all the nails on the wall, and he was proud of it. He ran to his dad and told him that he had pulled out all the nails, and he was now a different boy. The dad and the kid went to the wall and looked at it. The dad told the kid, "I am pleased to see that you have removed all the nails, and are getting positive compliments, but have you noticed one thing on the wall? It is never the same as before—even though all the nails got removed, the marks remain on the wall."

It is always good not to damage your reputation and then try to correct it. I have seen people who pay too much attention to their credit card minimum payments and bill payments to make sure their credit score is kept in good rating, while they are careless about society, or even the people they deal with directly, every day in their life. This kind of attitude would jeopardize their future success, big time.

People Want to Do Business With the Individuals Who Have a Good Reputation

Wherever you go, your previous behaviour is crosschecked for your future potentials. If you want to rent a place, the landlord will want to check with your previous landlords. When you apply for a new loan, the bank will want to check your credit history. When you apply for a new job, the new hiring company will want to do a reference check with the previous company, supervisors, and colleagues. When you want to do business with new people, they will want to check your past successful projects. Having a good reputation is a very powerful habit, which you should work hard to sharpen further and further.

Even though it was my last day at my job at Syntronic Canada, I have previously agreed to accompany the president, as well as the marketing manager of the company, to meet a prospective customer. They told me, since it was my last day, if I didn't want to go with them, they would be fine with that. I told them that I had promised to be part of it in the past, and I would be totally happy to go to the meeting with them. Even though I am not a marketing guy who can impress the customers with sweet talk, with my high level of positive energy, I was able to do my part to impress the customers with the company I was about to leave. Everyone was happy that the meeting was constructive. After I moved to Toronto from Ottawa, I was extremely busy with my real estate projects and unexpected issues. For sure, business has its ups and downs. After about six months, I got an email and, subsequently, a teleconference from my previous director at Syntronic, they offered me to take on a project in Japan, for three to four weeks, as a private consultant.

That enabled me to realize how much trust they had in me, even after I voluntarily left the company.

Keep the Promises, and Always Be There to Answer

As an entrepreneur, you would be required to raise capital to grow your business. If you are inventing something new, or starting a new business with just an idea, you would need seed money to organize and get your idea into action. Once you have partnered with investors, it is your responsibility to make sure the investor is up to date with the progress, or even the road blocks you will be encountering. It is a best practice to have periodic meet-ups or investor's sessions to have a detailed discussion about how the funds are getting used, and what progress is achieved towards the promised end results.

The investors should be treated with dignity, and their hard-earned money should be protected by any means. If it was your own money, and you did not make wise decisions, and you lost your money, that can be excused. In order to experiment your passionate idea, you spent your own time and money. Even if you lose your own money, and the idea was a failure, you have learned a wealth of knowledge during the course of execution.

It is always good to under-promise and, in reality, to over perform, rather than the other way around. I was partnering in an investment project, with an investors group, while living in Ottawa. The property was purchased in the Greater Toronto Area. I had invited one of the investment partners, who was living in Toronto, to view the property, and he was amazed. I had purchased the property for lower than the listed price, and it was a custom built good property on a large lot. I had promised that the ROI (Return on Investment) would be in the range of 15%. After two years, the annual ROI on that project was beyond 40%. All the investors were greatly appreciative, and executed a few more partnership projects with my company.

When the investment partners ask for clarification, don't get intimidated and avoid providing the info. Think of it as an opportunity to show them how good you are in terms of making wise decisions, executing projects in a timely manner, and keeping track of all the transactions. Once they receive the answers they were seeking, and the mind is clear, they would be delighted to do more business with you, or they would be the best referral for you.

Accept the Failure, and Share with Honesty

Not all venturous projects will be a success. I have even seen failures from companies that are over 100 years old, while companies that are only a few years old, flourish with success. In reality, a higher percentage of newer start-up companies fail, but you should not give up. If you have business partners or investment partners, before everyone commits to it, it is a best practice to sit down and analyze the pros and cons of the business. If you see more pros, and the hurdles can be overtaken with proper assistance, you could proceed with it. You should be a positive thinker and learn from the failures. Any failures will shape you into a better person. While collaborating with investment partners, if the new investment idea is running into issues, or has a higher chance to become a failure, it would be better off to explain the actual situation and the reason for the negative outcome. It could be an opportunity to bring in the stakeholders, and brainstorm ideas to think differently. The savvy investors always expect a certain percentage of failures, and they diversify their investments into multiple projects. They would be appreciative of the explanation they receive rather than being kept in the dark till the business closes down. This kind of practice may give you another chance for the same or future business adventures.

Increase Your Visibility

Meeting up with more likeminded people always energizes you in a positive way. When each one of you shares the great experience you have, it makes you feel good. At the same time, it may open up your mind to approach your business in a better way as per the ideas you have accumulated. The people who want to do business with you want to know you better. The chemistry has to work out between individuals in order to trust each other. Meeting many people in the area you are interested in would increase your chance of gaining more knowledge, getting invested in your business, and accumulating new ideas.

Sharing your knowledge is always a great thing rather than keeping it to yourself. It shows that you know what you are doing and are an expert on it. It will create confidence in you. You need to have a plan to meet potential investors or business people regularly to increase your chances. Doing everything yourself, and not knowing what is happening in the industry, would diminish your growth. Always be ready to accept new ideas, and appreciate others' efforts.

Any industries you are in, you have to interact with many businesses or individuals to get things successfully executed. Having a good relationship with suppliers and consultants is essential. It would be the best practice to get more introductions through your contacts, and so on. Even if someone kindly denied doing business with you at the time, ask if that same person knows someone who might be interested in doing business with you. I called one of my real estate contacts last month to do an investment project. My intention was to share a good opportunity and grow my projects. Unfortunately, he declined my offer due to his financial difficulties, but he told me that two of his good friends were highly interested in the kind of investment projects I do. Even though I had known them a long time, his referral reassured them to invest with me immediately, and we executed two real estate investment projects within two weeks.

People would rather do business and associate with a reputable and trustworthy person, than with someone who has lots of money through illicit activities. When your investment opportunity matches with other individuals' objectives, the collaboration takes place. As your reputation brings potential investors and partners into the business, being organized and having effective time management will accelerate your business.

Chapter 4

Organization and Time Management are Essential

Multi-tasking

While having a full time job, seeding a business idea, or starting a business at an early age, it requires discipline and effective management of time. Some youngsters may goof off while studying for the sake of their parents. Most adults go to work, come home, and browse the internet or watch TV. They have to go to work because of their basic needs of food and shelter. An entrepreneur should be able to do many things in parallel, or sequentially very effectively. When you have the drive to be an entrepreneur, you ought to have your own style of managing time wisely. If you stay away from negative conversations, that would save lot of valuable time. When an employee slacks around, and is involved in unnecessary negative conversations like group chats, personally, they don't lose much. They still get paid, and the job is still there for them. When an entrepreneur spends his or her time on such conversations, they lose their time, money, and motivation, and the end result could be the failure of their adventurous business idea.

If you are a student, make sure while focusing on your studies, try to experiment with your business ideas to get the feeling of running a business. It could be an online sale, garage sale, or creating small games, toys, or Apps—or anything. Make sure you don't lose your childhood too. Try to spend some quality time with your friends. No matter what, even with a billion dollars a single second, what we lose cannot be bought back. You need to have a planned agenda to achieve your goals each day, week, month, and year. First, you have to make sure your daily time management is done wisely. Some people think being on time somewhere, or finishing work ahead of time, is a way of having the best time management. Instead, I am a firm believer of rushing and ending up having a job half done, without proper cross-checking, just to attend an appointment way ahead of time and wait there for an hour, which is a total waste of time. You have to respect others' time, but at the same time, you have to maximize your daily achievements. If you wait at appointments for thirty minutes, and if the person you are supposed to meet runs late by fifteen minutes, for three appointments per day, it would cause you to lose two hours and fifteen minutes. Wow, that is almost twenty-five percent of your eight to ten working hours in a day. There are numerous ways to waste your time. Chatting with friends—and most of the time having negative conversations— would bring down your motivation. It is a good habit to avoid those conversations, or not be a part of it at all, which would be the best thing you could do for yourself.

I am writing this chapter while on my way to Tokyo, Japan, on an engineering consulting mission, of which I can guarantee that multi-tasking is critically important. I am going to be away for a week, but next month I am closing two venture partnership real estate acquisitions with my investment partners. I made sure my investment partners were notified of my departure, and I communicated with the closing lawyer and the mortgage broker, after providing all the required info. I even made sure all bill payments and cheque issuance were executed for upcoming payments. As an entrepreneur, you cannot leave any bases unsecured. Even if it is a noncritical transaction slip, you may end up paying a huge price down the road.

Be Organized

If you are a student, your teachers and your parents would love for you to be organized. It allows you to be efficient. Unorganized people spend a lot of time looking for things, which would look bad in front of others, as well as create lot of stress for the people they work with. When you run a business, if you keep your legal documents separate and categorized properly— finance documents, venture partner agreements, and tax documents—it would be easy for you to always go back and access them. I have sometimes seen business people bringing bags full of receipts, invoices, and half misplaced bills to an accountant during tax time. After they leave, the bookkeeper and the data entry person would say that most people are like that, and it will be a nightmare to get all of it sorted out in order to get their tax filed on time. If you inherit a business, a system would have been established by the person you are inheriting from. When you create everything from scratch, it is very difficult to hire people for everything, and establish an organized system.

You will be financially challenged at the beginning. In order to be successful at the beginning, you should be in a position to wear many hats. At the same time, never hesitate to hire the appropriate experts as short-term consultants till you have passed the transition period of being a non-profit start-up, to profitable business. If you want your business to grow big, you cannot be the bottle neck by being cheap. Being willing to spend the money where it is necessary is as critically important as minimizing the expenses. If you have to rent a place and hire people, make sure to get that executed as early as possible for your business to flourish.

Since all documents, these days, are stored in computers and data bases, you should have a uniform method to organize your file structure. If you store everything everywhere, it would be very difficult to access them. You can see how I structure my investment properties data storage folder in the following link: **www.fireyourjobbook.com**. Each property I acquire with my investment partners is treated as an independent business. In one instance, after I sent out the investment yearly report to four investors, one of them requested to see all the invoices for the expenses, in order to be satisfied. Since I have everything stored in a dedicated folder for that particular property, including all the expenses above ten dollars, which were executed via invoices or receipts, I have provided everything within 24 hours. After receiving all the invoices via Box account he was impressed and highly satisfied, and came back to be involved in two more projects so far. If you want to grow and operate a successful business, you have to be organized when you talk and execute things. If you are organized, analyzing a business deal is very easy as well. You have to have a method to analyze your deals, and be in a position to predict and market your potential return on your investment.

Meet Potential Investors

Bigger investment deals are put together collaboratively through investment partners. You should always have a habit of meeting new people and coming out of your own little group, where you may not be able to work with them in a business manner. I remember I was talking with my close friends, whom I have known for years and would go out with quite often, but I could not do business with them. The practicality is you may need to have two groups of people in your circle: one for having fun, family parties, and leisure purposes, and the other for brainstorming and doing joint venture partner projects. The second group would potentially bail you out when you are in trouble in your business.

I remember, after I Fired my job, I was remodeling two properties—one got executed, and the other one was supposed to be remodelled and sold in Toronto— but I had a cash shortage in the middle of the project, for $60 000. I knew none of my friends or family members could lend me that much money on short notice. Instead of selling one of my other properties, I have creatively raised $140 000, executed this remodeling project, and acquired an investment property. That was from one of my networking people, with whom I have established a business relationship. As long as there is a common genuine interest, with honesty, there are ways you can attract potential investment partners. Meeting new people every week, and weeding out the unnecessary ones, are critically important. Once you establish your clientele, with a good reputation and visibility to the general public, the investors will be after you.

One of my mentors used to say that if you have a periodic meeting with potential investors or business partners, something may eventually happen. Either these individuals may do business with you, or introduce you to others. Everyone works hard to earn their savings. It would be very difficult for someone to easily give away their savings to someone else. It takes time for people to trust you and let the money work for them through your creative projects. I encountered a great experience last year. I knew this friend of mine for over twenty years, and he knows how savvy I am. He would sometimes approach me for real estate related advice, and I genuinely wanted him to be involved in real estate projects and get the benefit out of it. One day, I called him and said "I have a great opportunity; you could achieve better than 15% annual return on investment, and I will make sure, legally, that your investment funds will be secured, even if I die in an accident." He said he really wanted to be involved but, at that moment, he was financially stuck. He did not stop there but continued, and said, "I have four friends who really like what you do, and they might be interested." I respected his situation and told him we would do a deal when he was comfortable and ready. That night, he connected me with his four friends and, even without meeting three of them, they committed to do projects with me. We have executed many more since. It does not matter, rich or poor, having a good relationship with business potentials, and letting the others know your business growth and success, is more critically important than spending thousands of dollars on marketing to strangers at the beginning.

For the past nine years, I have given many real estate acquisitions and sales business to my lawyer, every year. He knows me well and, for me, his team would turn things around, even with 24-hours' notice. We were chatting freely after a private money lending, and he commented that this transaction seemed to be slightly higher interest with the initial fee. I had already analyzed that transaction; instead of complaining about higher interest and not doing a deal, as long as you would still make a profit as per your numbers, you should be ok. As you know, lawyers charge a lot of money, and they deal with wealthy clients. They do not have much interest in dealing with poor people, from a business point of view. An idea popped in my mind to pick his brain. I told him, "Yes, I do understand it is a bit higher in interest; and as you know, my business is growing with multiple venture partners. Do you think you may have clients you could introduce me to, to do business with? I should be able to get them a good return on investment, and the capital would be secured." He immediately said, "I do have clients who would be interested in doing business with you, and you don't need to pay the additional percentage of fees you just paid." Wow, it is mind blowing, isn't it? You never know where your future business partners or leads are hiding. Always keep your eyes and ears open, and be ready to capitalize it.

Procrastination

Many people are stuck because of procrastination. The definition of procrastination, from Webster's dictionary, is "to put off intentionally the doing of something that should be done." Instead of sending an investor report or analysing a deal, you may end up checking Facebook or your WhatsApp messages, or you may even tweet something. You think you will only be a few minutes, but you would have easily already spent 30 minutes. I have a habit of checking the news quickly, for 5 to 10 minutes, in a predetermined period of time, while starting my day. I found it was consuming way more than what I had promised myself. The reason is, when you read news in the media, they seldom bring news that would motivate people. The media and the news channels, either online or on TV, bring all sorts of negative news, which you have no control over or have nothing to do with. Their business model works perfectly because most of the viewers are flocking to that kind of product. My personal experience is that you don't waste the amount of time you spend reading the news or watching it, but your mind would still remember and get distracted. It will bring down your productivity. It is always good to be disciplined, and achieving what you ought to achieve on a set date is critical for your end results. You must stop satisfying yourself doing noncritical tasks and putting off the critical ones that are absolutely necessary.

Be Unique and Stand Out

In your business, when you are unique compared to the majority of your competitors, it will enable you to stand out. You don't want to be one of many trying to do business in the same manner as others. I remember, in the early nineties, the first computer I used was an Apple INC. Macintosh computer. It was very user-friendly compared to the competition, even 25 years ago, with Graphical User Interphase (GUI). It was very easy to use, while an early version of Windows had so much trouble with DOS prompts to execute many operations. Apple also came into the mobile phone world very late, compared to Motorola, Palm Pilot, Nokia, and Blackberry. Blackberry was the pioneer in the smart phone business, with higher security features and the key board. Steve Jobs (Apple's CEO) introduced the smart phone very late in the game, but with unique features. He put so much emphasis on user interface and the slickness of the smart phone he had introduced, that it became a sensation.

I remember when I was flying on business trips, in the mid-2000s, and if you carried a Blackberry phone, people were thinking you were in a management or executive role. These days, almost everyone is carrying an Apple or a Samsung phone, and the early players got wiped out. In a business, if you are not unique and serve the customers, you will not last long. When many people are drowning, if you are trying to get help in a similar way to others above the water level, you will have less chance of getting help. If you wave your hand high above the others, you will be noticed, and most likely you will be pulled out from the water.

Don't feel shy about being different from others. If you are an out-of-the box thinker, you may run into confrontations at work, or with others on collaborative tasks. It is good to be different, as long as you bring valuable thoughts and ideas to the table. Some people listen to everyone, and don't object to anything; they pretend to be very easy going. Since they are not listened to, they suffer a lot themselves. At the same time, they lack creativeness. When I was quitting my six-figure salary job, with flexible hours, most of my family members, friends, and colleagues thought I was crazy. Nothing made me change my mind from having my own venture and determining my own destiny, on my own terms. Since I have been in the engineering industry for over 20 years, and have a wealth of unique experience as a RF Designer, finding a job is very easy for me. Instead, I do part-time technical engineering consulting, while focusing on developing my own business, and I can make the same salary as when I was an employee, in less than six months. In a year, I am able to free up 50% of my time by doing this.

If you are a student or an employee, feel free to express your good ideas, and train yourself to be unique from others. Don't get too comfortable with what you do. Get out there and get into action.

Chapter 5

Time is Limited – Don't Get Too Comfortable

Life Is Too Short – Act Fast

The world lasts millions of years, but as mature and healthy adults, in Canada, we have an average lifespan of approximately 82 years. During this time, if we sit around too much, it would be a waste of life time. We should have a more meaningful life than just a repetitive, typical life. If you are a student or a worker, you should push your capability at least ten percent higher, to exceed your limit. As soon as you get comfortable in that new state, you should again push it another ten percent higher. This is how, without too much stress to yourself, you could raise your bar higher and higher. Some people could increase their capability by 50% each year, and achieve their target faster than others.

You have only 24 hours in a day; even within that, you may only get 8 to 10 quality hours to work on whatever it is that you do. I remember, some of my close associates would say, "I go to work, and that is very important for me. At work, I get time to relax and chat with colleagues, have a coffee, have lunch out, and all sorts of things." I could clearly see these individuals were not challenged at all, and were too comfortable in the state where they were at. They had not tried using their full capability to achieve their goals. Most people, when they are challenged, get motivated, and would be more creative.

If you are a student, you don't have to stop with just the homework and the projects. These days, the Internet is flooded with information, and you could study something more on your own, ahead of time, to get higher marks and expand your wealth of knowledge. There are even opportunities just while staying at home; you could experiment with online businesses. Even if you fail at it, your loss would be very minimal. At an early age, if you lose financially, it would be very less, and the experience would shape you in the future as a better business person. At the same time, when you lose later in life, the loss would be higher, and it would be very hard to correct yourself and retrieve it back.

I remember one of my colleagues, while I was working at Blackberry; even after working in the high tech industry for over 30 years, he would work hard and was concerned about his job. One day, I was talking with him, and said, "You have been in the industry, with a high-paying job for over thirty years, and you should be financially okay and ready to retire soon." He looked at me, and said, "Sorry, Akilan; I have three kids, and they are almost finished university. They are also living with me, and I lost lots of money in the stock market with the Dot Com crash in the 2000s, after 911. It looks like, if my health permits, I may need to work beyond my retirement age." At the time I was talking with him, he was nearly 60. I was in my mid- 30s, and dreaming of when to Fire my JOB, while this poor guy was thinking about working beyond his retirement age. We both lost a lot of money in the Dot Com crash. At the time, I was beginning to invest, but his investment was arms and legs for him. Even I lost most of my savings at the time, but early age lessons directed me into different strategies, and I was able to recoup the loss in a matter of years, with another measured risk-taking investment strategy. At a young age, you have high energy and enthusiasm, and you have to maximize it. Many people assume the successful people are geniuses, or they inherited wealth from their parents. Those are lame excuses to be lazy. There are more self-made millionaires than the millionaires who inherited the money. Being determined, with a never-give-up attitude, brought many entrepreneurs to success.

Be Dynamic to Accept the Changes and Reshape the Strategies

If you could be open to new ideas, and develop a thirst for learning new things, your decision-making would be wiser, and could be accepted by many people. I lost thousands of dollars by investing in the stock market right after graduating from university. At the time, I had no clue about investment, or even about the stock market. Since I am the first immigrant to Canada, unfortunately I could not rely on someone for advising me. If I would have given up getting actively involved in investments, I would not have been able to recover the loss, and gain multifold investments, and create my own business. When you run into obstacles, right away if you look for an alternative path to achieve your target, there will be multiple routes. Instead, many people get stuck with the same method of approach to their issues; they work hard to break that obstacle, and then fail or give up. You might be persistent and determined, but the economic conditions and the others you rely on could change anytime, without any warning. During these times, you should be flexible enough to change your direction to make sure there will be a minimum impact in your targeted outcome.

While you rise above the normal crowd, you will encounter obstacles, failures, betrayals, and lots of stress. Instead of standing on the ground, when you climb up the ladder, you are more exposed as you reach the top. We only know the success stories of the entrepreneurs, but not many people know the suffering they had gone through to achieve their success, which is known to the whole world. When you go through tough issues, you may think that it is the end of the world. Once you resolve that issue and move on with it, you would feel much stronger than before. It is good to go through issues earlier than later in your business.

No Need to Be a Lone Wolf

When you start a new business, you should know what the outcome would be and where to start. There will be numerous tasks that may need to be taken care of to shape up the business and run it successfully. You should start delegating the tasks and learn to let the jobs go that can be done by others. You may know almost everything, but you don't need to be the one implementing it. When you focus on the tasks that only you can do, it would make you an expert on that, and it would be critical for your business. At the beginning, you could start hiring appropriate experts, even on a contract basis; then, as you start making revenue, start to hire full-time employees. If you make the mistake of taking care of the small tasks, and not taking enough time to educate yourself and focus on the tasks only you could do for the business, it will jeopardise the growth of the business, and create unnecessary stress.

Crave for Challenges

In order for you to raise your capability, you have to constantly challenge yourself and stimulate your brain. When you do a repetitive job, your brain won't get stimulated, and will lack creativeness. If you are an employee, it is better to communicate with your superior to get feedback, and to move into a more responsible role than what you have been doing for a long time. If you are an entrepreneur, make sure to expand your business to the next level every year. Even if you don't have the capability to execute a new or bigger project, have a game plan; once you have started executing it, you will find many ways as you progress. If you sit with cold feet, it would be very difficult to move forward and achieve your goals. You have to be a role model for your employees.

I had a phone call from Darrell Wellington, the director of engineering at my former place of employment. He asked me to go to Japan for one week as a consultant, due to some issues needing to be enhanced for a product I had designed in the past. I was out of touch for almost a year with the engineering details. I had kind of denied his request in the past due to my busy schedule and not being able to go on a slightly longer-term mission. Since I did not want to turn him down again, I told him not to worry, and that I was in and ready to book the flight ticket. I know he had full faith in me and was confident that I could handle it. Even so, I promised him I would make sure, whatever the issue, I would take care of it. In reality, I did not know the technical details of the issue they were having, nor did I have the proper software tools on my laptop to even communicate with the system, but I felt that I could do it. My wife said to me, "You have been out of touch for a while with the engineering activities; make sure you can resolve the issue they have." My only answer to her was: "I Do Not Accept Failure As A Result."

I went there and utilized the team, in Japan, to assist me where I was out of touch, and I rapidly ramped up in a few hours. I had teleconferences with the Ottawa team, and all the issues got resolved within three solid days. Initially, I was asked to go on this trip for two weeks. Due to my real estate business, I had only committed to a week. Towards the end of the week, the project manager and the program managers, from Ericsson, Japan, met with me. They said the product exceeded their expectations in design, and that I performed a miracle to resolve the issue, and they were very pleased. The Ottawa Syntronic management team had also praised me for being persistent and determined. As per my experience, Japanese people are very polite, respectful, and cooperative; at the same time, they are very determined and demanding. When you commit something to them, you had better be more than one hundred percent committed. What I want you to know is, if I would have sat in my house trying to see what necessary steps would be needed to resolve their issue, and how I was going to do it, I would not have had any answers. When your confidence is high, and you are full of commitment, miracles can happen.

A Typical Lifestyle Doesn't Get You Anywhere

If you are striving for success, you have to come out of your typical life style, and start doing something different that is out of your comfort level. When I was working at Nortel Networks,

I would come home, have supper, and then sit in front of the TV and watch shows till I went to bed, around 10 pm. I would start with Friends, or Everybody Loves Raymond, and I would even watch The Simpsons, at 9 pm. I did not realize I was wasting my time doing nothing. I was too comfortable at the time: I was working for a great Canadian engineering firm; I felt it would last forever; and, most likely, I would have career growth, and retire from there. When I was walking into the Nortel building, in Kanata, Ottawa, it was a totally different feeling. I never felt that amazing feeling in any other company. My time, and most of my invested money, also went into Nortel Networks. They went through numerous rounds of layoffs, but I survived. I told myself that it was a research company that started over one hundred years ago, and it would come around.

In August, 2001, I went to Europe on a vacation. After I returned from my vacation, I noticed there was a voice message from my manager, asking me to meet him as soon as I got back. I realized something wasn't right. When I met with him, he told me, "You have been a great employee, and we would love to keep you, but as you know, the company is not doing great, and we are shutting down the whole division you are in; here is the package to leave." He offered to help me in any way, and he even gave me a list of his own high-tech engineering contacts, whom I could contact to apply for jobs.

That day was the worst day of my career life. I did not talk to anyone; I just went and slept. All my dreams were shattered like broken glass, and it was so terrible. Losing a job for the first time since graduating and working as a professional, was the worst thing. The next day, I woke up early in the morning and started to apply for jobs; within two weeks, I had landed another job.

Nortel gave me severance pay at the time, with two months' continued biweekly salary payments, and then a package. For one and a half months, I had two high-tech incomes, instead of one. My experience in numerous companies led me to not get too comfortable but to create my own destiny.

Stop Continuous Small Talk

Average people enjoy talking about politics or war, and issues around the world. They would even spend so much time listening, watching, and reading about it. They don't realize those activities don't bring food to the table or pay their kids' tuition fees; instead, it brings down their positive energy. For an example, when you meet your colleague at the coffee stand, or while waiting for the elevator, or even at the airport, think about what you do or normally talk about. Many people, these days, get in the habit of burying themselves in their smart phones, without even realizing who is beside them. For business people, they use small talk as an ice breaker to initiate the conversation; then, within a few minutes, they will switch to talking about business, or something beneficial for both parties. This may potentially lead to future business or some other introductions. They even get ideas for a new business, or pick others' brains to brainstorm an idea.

I was sitting at the Tokyo Haneda Airport, waiting to be boarded, when I saw a lady on her phone, texting to someone or checking her emails. I had trouble connecting to the airport WIFI connection, and I thought about asking her if she managed to get the WIFI connected easily. I started my small talk by saying hi to her, and then genuinely asked if she had any issue connecting to the WIFI. She responded to me by saying that she lives in Tokyo, and she has the local SIM card to use it. That was an interesting thing for me; unlike North America or Europe, I saw very few foreigners there during my stay. I asked her if she permanently moved to Japan and planned to retire there. She said that she and her husband were going to retire in a few years, and they were planning to buy a property near Toronto Canada for their future stays. After I explained her that I do engineering consulting these days, while focusing most of my time developing my business into real estate, she was so glad that we had a chat—she asked for my business card to meet up. This is a very good example how, without any marketing and traveling to meet someone, I had a business meet-up, at no cost. If I would have stayed silent and took a nap, or even just continued my small talk, it would not have been fruitful for either of us.

Create Your Own System, and Follow

In your business, having a proven system is critically important for your long-term success. Once you identify which system is working the best, you could train your employees to follow and execute it the way in which you would. If they could execute it with minor changes that would enhance your pattern, it would be great, but make sure they don't deviate in a negative way. When I started to invest in real estate, I did not have a system to identify, analyze, acquire, manage, remodel, or renovate and calculate the profit centres. As time passed by, after executing a few deals, I created my own system for everything. It became part of me. Later, I even purchased deals without even seeing the properties.

Now, my investors are purchasing properties, relying on my system, and they don't even visit their investment properties. When it comes to deal structuring my investment acquisitions, my lawyer and his staff are now educated, and they know how to execute it. Whatever business you are in, try your ideas with measured risk. If that idea fails, be willing to accept the loss, and move on with the other one. Some of your ideas may work for a while, and then it may not be viable for long term. In this case, dynamically, you have to make the appropriate changes and reshape and redirect it. Once it is proven to be working seamlessly, keep doing more of what is successful for you.

Living too comfortable, without realizing your full capacity, is something you should avoid. You have to make sure your purpose for living is fulfilled with your actions, and not sabotaged by fear and comfort. People talk about being frustrated and don't know what to do. Let's talk about how to turn your frustration into your success.

Chapter 6

Frustration Is Good to Have

Frustrated by the Stock Market (Loss)

I started to work in high-tech industry, in 1999, at the company called Nortel Networks. I was so excited to be part of the high paying, high technological, and corporate world. At the time, the stock market, for technology companies, was sky rocketing. In those days, during coffee breaks and at any gatherings, people were talking about how much the technology stocks were growing, and the lucrative yield they were getting. Nortel was a Canadian, multinational, iconic company, established over 100 years ago. Even though I had a student loan at the time, I had started to invest in technology stocks and registered retirement savings plan (RRSP) funds were also got invested with Nortel Networks. At the peak, it employed close to 100 000 employees. No one taught me how to invest or follow any strategies in stock trading. Unfortunately, I was the first generation in Canada, and I was just out of university, trying to establish myself.

The Dot com crash took place in November 2000. Trillions of dollars were lost during that time. Nortel Network's stocks were going down, day by day. I started to think about averaging down the holdings I had. I kept on buying, even after I got laid off in 2001. A couple of other technology companies, which I had invested in, went bankrupt. I had purchased thousands of Nortel stocks, betting on an over one-hundred-year-old, well-established company to come back. The worst thing was, the executives from the company were still drawing retaining bonuses. Eventually, in 2009, Nortel Networks also filed bankruptcy. I was devastated that I lost my first high paying engineering job, and all my retirement savings with Nortel Networks got wiped out, and the externally invested stocks also went down to nothing. Thank God, I never had any issue finding another job.

Once I was in the job market looking for a job, within a few weeks or days, I was with another technology company. I took that as a lesson learned, and realized that my investment had to be under my control rather than letting someone else control it. During that search, I found real estate investment as the avenue to achieve my goal. If I would have thought about running a small business, I would either have had to hire people to run it, or I would have to spend my day operating the small business. When I was going through that rough time, it was complete frustration. Now, when I look back, I am glad it happened, and I learned it earlier in my life than later. It is always good to try, and fail, earlier than later, because the financial loss, and time lost are minimal. Another thing is, when you are young, you won't give up easily. You will have the energy to fight back—to climb up the ladder again.

Frustrated by the Layoffs

Sometimes getting laid off from a company is good. My first lay off from Nortel Networks was so sad. I used to work in the huge research centre, in the Ottawa west end, where they had thousands of engineering employees, with fancy facilities and perks. I was thinking, at the time, "Wow, that's it; this is the company I am going to work for till I retire. I am settled." I had started to get comfortable, but the Dot Com crash impacted my career as well. The second lay off, from the start-up company called Spotwave Wireless, was so interesting. I was working at this start-up company as a product engineer, and I was wearing many hats to substantially contribute to the success of the company. At the time, I was given 50 000 stock options, at the price of CDN $0.05. I had calculated, if the company went public, and if the stock price reached $20, I could become a millionaire. During this time I wanted to take my financial status to the next level, so I made a deposit to build my first house in Ottawa, Canada.

Again, the unfortunate situation came up: Spotwave had some financial difficulties. They forced me to take a forty percent pay cut, and to work just three days per week. That was a hit in the forehead. At the time, I had no choice, other than finding another job. Within a few weeks, I got a better offer from another start-up company. Once I told my management that I had found another full time paying opportunity, and was quitting my job, they would not accept my resignation. In a start-up company, all the employees are important, and I was holding a key position within the product development team—I was the only one performing certain tasks as a one-man army. They asked me what I needed; they didn't want the answer that I was leaving the company. I pinched myself for a moment to be sure this was really happening. I requested that I be sent out for a one-week training, which I had already asked for but had got denied. I had not had any training in the last couple of years for the technology I was working with. Poof! It was granted that I attend a seminar in San Jose, California, for a week, with all the expenses to be covered by the company. Besides that, I was offered a retaining stock option bonus, and a salary increase of roughly 20%.

In the corporate world, it does not matter how hard you work or how much you contribute; at the end of the day, you are a head count. If they need to cut operating costs, and don't need your services, you will be out the door. Eventually, Spotwave Wireless ran into financial difficulties again and had to lay me off. After the second one, I started to embrace the layoffs. The day I got laid off, I told my wife I was glad I got laid off and got the severance pay. Instead of sitting in a corner and wondering why this happened to me, I would wake up early in the morning and apply for jobs. Within a week, I landed a job at Blackberry. At that time, when I joined the company, it was called Research in Motion—another Canadian telecommunication company that was one of the early smart phone pioneers.

While I was working at Blackberry, even though things were fine, my instinct warned me not to get comfortable, and to start to have an alternative financial backup. I told myself, enough is enough, and I cannot be scared of losing jobs again. In 2008, I started to research what to invest and where to invest. Even though I was living in Ottawa, I bought my first investment property, in 2009, in one of the best neighbourhoods in Toronto. This was the time that a real estate crash had taken place in the US, and Canada had witnessed a moderate slow down. I used this opportunity, with my previous severance pay and investment partners, to acquire my first, out-of-town investment property. If you are a confident individual, and have a game plan, the best opportunity is while everyone is scared. When I look for investment properties, I look for the properties that weren't loved enough, and would be hated by most people.

When I was comfortably working, I started to accumulate a portfolio of properties across Ontario, Canada, one after another. Eventually, the big pay day came with another layoff from Blackberry, in 2014. I was so excited to be laid off; I used the capital from the layoff payment to buy a four-plex apartment building, in Windsor, Ontario. I sold that property this year, and made CDN $110 000 as net profit. Again, I utilized this capital, and reinvested in three different properties, with investment partners. Now, my layoff package money keeps on growing, and got diversified. Instead of you working hard, you have to let your money work hard for you.

After the layoff from Blackberry, within a week, I became a consultant rather than being an employee. This self-promotion increased my consulting fee by 50% more than what I was earning before. Don't ever get negatively frustrated from getting let go by the companies. It could create a forced opportunity to reconsider the way you operate, and the services you provide. If you are running a small business, it is better to have loss than having just enough income that would pay your salary. In this case, you are not running a business: it would be a job for you. If you run into loss, then you will get proper help outside, or re-strategize your business practice to overcome the loss in a better way. Instead of negatively getting frustrated, I have turned my frustration energy into positive actions that would get me out of the biweekly pay cheque dependency.

Frustrated by Senior Management's Lack of Vision

The unfortunate situation is that you may work for a great reputable company, but if you are not an executive, or in a senior management role, you will be directed by someone else. That individual who holds the management role may sometimes act to achieve their own interest rather than the corporate vision. If you don't deliver what they have asked you to, even though that misaligns the company target, you will be labelled as a person who does not deliver the assigned tasks. On a few occasions, I had to stand up and clearly state to my manager that I would not do things that would be unethical and would potentially bring loss to the company I was working for. In order to do this, it requires lots of self-confidence. At the same time, it has created a lot of frustration.

I have seen numerous corporate failures occur due to a lack of vision by the senior management team, or they fail to indicate that the CEO is on the wrong path. If the CEO was a founder, and was attached to the company emotionally, he may not think outside the box after a while. Of course, the founder created the company from nothing, and it has grown to a certain level where it became successful. After internally working so long, they may lose steam. When they hire executives, he or she assumes the new hires are going to be his or her eyes and ears for the company's growth; but instead, some of them start to suck up, and keep a practice of milking the existing products.

I have witnessed in a company, which I was working for, where they were making a lot of money (in the billions), and they were releasing the repetitive, multiple products, with less creativity. There was a situation where even the designers, who were designing the consumer product, did not like it because it lacked creativity. The instruction from the senior management team was given to deliver that product. Eventually, after releasing it to the customer, that product wasn't well received by the consumers, and it became a failure. It did not fail because the engineers did something wrong. It failed because the features, requested by the senior management team to deliver, lacked the creativity. Many corporate failures occur due to lack of long-term vision by the senior management team. It was a frustration because, due to someone above you made the mistake, and the company went into loss—you don't get a bonus and, eventually, the corporation has to go through cost cutting and layoffs. These kinds of occurrences are not under your direct control, but your alternate financial plan should go into full force now.

Frustrated by the Corporate Politics (Inner and Outer Circles)

Have you ever wondered why you are working as hard as your peers, and are dedicated to the company, but you don't have as many promotions, or even appreciation, during the performance reviews? Don't worry, you are not all alone; I have personally went through this under a few managements, and even assisted a few of my friends to find alternative opportunities at different companies. Some insecure managers try to have a few preferred people within their inner circle, while they leave others in the outer circle. The inner circle people would get promotions and good performance reviews, compared to the others. That would frustrate you, big time, because of the unethical behaviour of those particular managers. If you ever encounter a situation like that, don't put yourself down and think you are not a capable person. Instead, just do what needs to be done at work, and don't bother with the corporate politics. Now you should be more energized to focus on your alternate plan to be financially independent.

Some employees are better at sucking up to their superiors than actually performing well for the company. Those people survive by being nice to their superiors and following instructions blindly. When someone executes someone's orders without analyzing it, if that idea wasn't correct, the company ends up paying for the loss of time and the resources lost. When I ran into issues like that, I put extra effort into my side projects, and gained three times the bonus I would have received from the company I was working for. It all depends on how you approach the situation. When someone treats you badly, you are not obliged or expected to go the extra mile to provide your services. You should take that as a great opportunity to put all your extra energy into your own projects.

Turn Frustrated, Negative Energy into Positive Energy That Is Beneficial for You, Your Investment Partners, and Your Own Business

When you get frustrated due to a lack of appreciation at work, or by worrying about getting laid off, now you have a true purpose: to build your own independent business. Turning the uncomfortable, negative frustration into positive motivation would be the greatest thing you could ever do for yourself and the people who depend on you. Rather than getting depressed and letting yourself down, you should be fired up and full of energy. When someone says they are comfortable and everything is great, there is no energy to transform into another form. Those individuals are like the majority who accept the situation and live with it, or they just go with the flow, feeling incapable. At the same time, they would pretend everything is good. Getting frustrated, discussing the situation with superiors, and improving yourself, or taking on challenging tasks, would pave a path to climb up the corporate ladder.

When you work hard on your projects, with dedication, it would attract more investors to be part of it. It is a direct positive result you would create for yourself and your investment partners. Even when friends or colleagues give you negative comments, just don't let those negative comments control you. You should focus on your long-term goal, and take appropriate steps to achieve it. You will learn the purpose, and what you have to do to accomplish your goal, in the upcoming chapter.

Chapter 7

What? Why? How?

Decide What You Need to Achieve

There is no harm in dreaming to achieve certain things in life, but make sure you follow your dream to achieve it. There are people who have had higher imaginative dreams, and they achieved huge things in their life: Apple INC. founder, Steve jobs; Tesla founder, Elon Musk; and Amazon founder, Jeff Bezos, are very good examples from the present years. You have to decide what you want to achieve. There are people who have never spent their time to identify what they wanted to achieve in their life. It does not matter what your financial status is, you have to dream about your future achievement, and decide. You may have an ambition to live a lavish life in a nice, big, custom-built house, and drive an expensive vehicle. If that is your true purpose, take appropriate steps to achieve your goal. If you have kids, you may think about saving enough funds for the kids' education. If you are a person who likes visiting new places, and enjoys the different cultures, you may want to have multiple vacations. My initial goal was to be financially independent from being trapped in the biweekly paycheque dependency. My final ambition was to be a successful entrepreneur. I worked nights and weekends to fulfill my dream. The interpersonal skills, which I have discussed before, would come into play here, in assistance to reach your destination. Sit down peacefully, and think wisely. Analyze your current situation, and make a firm decision on what you want to achieve. This single decision will dictate your future actions.

Why Do You Need to Achieve?

Once you have decided on what you want to achieve in your life, you have to ask yourself why you are trying to achieve it. If you don't have a valid reason, the decision you made regarding what to achieve, may have a difficult time getting fulfilled. If you are a student, you may want to pass all your subjects with good marks; your parents would be proud of you, and you could get a good job once you finish your schooling. There are many people who want to quit their daytime job because, for them, they have a passion somewhere else. For the majority, the day-to-day job is not their passion. They are not too sure if they could generate revenue out of their passion. Since they do not want to take the risk, they stick with their day-to-day job. Your reasoning should be much bigger than just the direct impact on your own family and yourself. When your reasoning is big, and beyond your immediate family, the drive to achieve would have higher energy, and will get support from outside.

How to Achieve

Now, you have decided what to achieve, and why you are trying to achieve it. The actual implementation begins to fulfill your dream. It is a critical stage, and the mistakes you make will jeopardise your goal. Make sure to have a detailed, step-by-step process to slowly achieve your dream. Learn to accept that things don't happen overnight. There will be roadblocks and stressful situations; people you know may betray you or backstab you. Take every struggle as a lesson learned. Make sure to treat each obstacle as a life lesson, and learn from it to tackle things better in the future. All the losses you may encounter, you should treat them as tuition fees. If you change your thinking process, you won't be depressed or scared of obstacles.

Defining the vehicle to achieve your goal is also important. You may think about investing in stocks, mutual funds, private lending, and other means of investments. You could invest in real estate, and hold, or rehabilitate and flip. Down the road, you could even become a home builder. You could even start a small business, or have a big vision, and form a technology or production company, hoping to grow big.

If you are creating your own business from scratch, don't struggle by yourself. Give away a portion of your equity, and bring in the right resources to move fast. Instead of having 100% ownership, and not taking it anywhere, give away a certain percentage of the ownership to accelerate the success, which would be great. If you need proper training or education on the area of the business you will be creating, be willing to spend the money and the time. You could also educate yourself by reading books written by experts. Some times when you read books, it may not give you the direct advice or process to implement the techniques in your business. It would expand your thinking process and accumulate more knowledge in the subject matter.

I was determined to increase my wealth, which would be my backup during the loss of biweekly paycheques, through accumulating income producing properties. I also acquired properties that could be remodeled to force the value, to sell it for a higher price. Make sure to write up a plan, and define your medium to achieve your financial target.

Establish Your Timeline

Corporations spend lots of money on hiring trained project managers, coordinators, and program managers to make sure each project is managed properly to meet the final deadline. Most of the time, these individuals won't have the direct experience to actually implement or execute the ground level tasks, but they define every step in the process, from the beginning till the end. You have to do the same thing: have a blueprint of what your first step should be, and how long it is going to take. Your subsequent steps should be defined too. You have to revisit your plan, every three months, to dynamically change as per your progress. If you are stuck and not moving anywhere, identify the root cause, and find a solution for it. Don't be a slacker in your own project. Start to feel guilty if you did not meet your own milestone. You should have your own deadlines, and be accountable.

Start to Market Earlier Than Later

Don't start to prematurely release all the details of your potential technology business idea or plans to others, and brag about it. Work on it, and discuss it with the appropriate people— they could be part of it or could give you guidance. At the same time, once your business project is launched from a solid foundation, and while it progresses as you have planned, don't keep it under the rug anymore. Slowly, you have to test the market by discussing it with people whom you may do business with in the future. That may bring some ideas to reshape your business. It will also help in building your clientele. Don't spend money on marketing till the business is in a matured stage to handle clients.

I was very busy with my full-time engineering job and real estate projects. Even though I had a great idea in my mind two years ago, I did not have the time to proceed with it. This year, in September, after all the competitive research, I finally decided to launch the business. Now, I have a team of two in Ottawa and Toronto, working to get the product released. I am writing this chapter on Halloween, in 2017. I have already started to talk to a few people in multiple cities, and even overseas, for the potential usage. I have a friend in the UK with whom I have discussed the services my company will be providing, and he said he wished a service like that existed in the UK. When I was talking with my investor friend in Montreal, Canada, I briefly explained to him that I am working on a product that would be a marketing service for anyone who does any kind of business in real estate. He got excited, and told me, "Aks, once the solution is available, let me know. I want to use it as soon as the product is released." I am hoping the solution I am going to provide will be well received, and would be a great success. At the same time, from multiple people, I have already received great positive feedback. They have not even seen the product yet. Now, I am building my customers slowly, and keeping the excitement going. Once the product is ready, it would be an easy introduction to these people.

I admire Microsoft for selling a multi-billion dollar Windows product that may require further enhancements, and then sending the patches after the release. They had already built the clientele, and the people were accepting it as is, and then were willing to accept the updates at a later time. If they could do it, why do you have to wait till the last perfect day? Just get out there and slowly build your client base, and understand how well your idea is received in the market. It is easier to reshape or improve your product sooner than later. Reshape your business strategies from the trustworthy and dependable people's feedback, and keep marching forward. Ignore the people who may give you negative feedback without any facts.

In order for you to reach the finish line, your brain has to be with you. Let's talk about how to keep yourself engaged and have positive energy. The positive energy you would get from like-minded people is also crucial.

Chapter 8

Educate and Surround Yourself with Like-Minded People

Educate Yourself

We spend a number of years (probably around 18 years) from the time we start to learn, till we graduate from university, and find a job. This education we go through could be somehow more focused by the time we graduate from university or college. Still, once you start to work, or have your own business, it could be a bit outdated, or won't give you the direct knowledge you would require to excel your day-to-day performance. At the same time, when the companies hire you, they are not willing to spend their time and money to get you trained. Since they are paying from the day you start to work, they are expecting you to produce a required outcome as soon as possible. How many of us educate ourselves during the off time, or spend more time and money to educate in the relevant field? I don't think many of us do that, due to various reasons; we find excuses not to do it. If you want to be an entrepreneur, you have to feed your brain with knowledge. Some people focus a lot on hands-on experience, and then they submerge themselves, not thinking out of the box. For an example, if you are a good mechanic, and want to open a mechanic shop, you must already be a very good mechanic. You may pose a number of years of experience in handling various models of cars, and dealing with customers. Before you start to open up your business, you have to learn a lot about managing employees, and handling all matters, starting from legal, finance to organizational management. Instead of focusing mostly on the technical aspect, and always thinking of yourself as another technician, your focus should be broader, and of big picture thinking. It is time for you to wisely allocate resources, and manage the finances properly. If you think you would save money by putting in your own hours as a mechanic, then your business will have less chance for growth and prosperity.

You could always read books about relevant entrepreneurial experience from others. Attending part-time courses would also enrich you. As per Statistics Canada, a business with 1 to 100 employees falls under the small business category; meanwhile, in the US, up to 500 employees would be considered as a small business. The astonishing thing is that the small businesses employ more than 90% of the total workforce in Canada and the United states. Unfortunately, even though small businesses are the critical part of the economy, we don't see entrepreneurship education in high schools or universities. It is your responsibility to get relevant education and become a successful business person, than finding another job as working for yourself.

Attend Meet-up Groups and Seminars

Your time is finite; use it wisely. When you are running a start-up company, your family's, employees' and company's financial future depends on you. Make sure you're doing the things that only you can do, and delegate the rest. Attending seminars and meet-up groups are highly critical for small business entrepreneurs to widen their knowledge. I remember, I was attending the meet-up groups in Ottawa, every month, while I was having issues with one of my tenants in Toronto. One day, there was a panel discussion to discuss the landlord and tenant matters. During this panel discussion, I was able to identify a key point that I was able to use against my troublesome tenant, and finally evict him out of my rental property. It saved me thousands of dollars, and that particular headache was gone forever. In your local areas, there will also be meet-up groups, or you could even attend out-of-town seminars. Getting out of your local area, and attending the out-of-town meet-up groups to meet people from other areas, would sometimes expose you to a totally different world. Successful people like sharing their great path of success, with pride. Your actions are controlled by you, and your mind is everything. When you are motivated, you can go beyond your comfort zone and execute things that you may be surprised at when you look back. When you are demotivated, you lack on executions. As a result, you may not make appropriate decisions at the right time, and it may pave a path for a loss in your business, or even hinder your growth potential. Sometimes the experience, or the way of business executions others share, may not be able to directly apply in your geographic location or in your unique business. As long as you learn to modify and transform the idea to work best for you, your success is certain.

While you are attending meet-up groups, you get the chance to explain your business to others, and pitch your ideas to get funded. When you pitch your ideas, you may get criticism from experts in a similar field, or from the people who potentially wanted to invest in it. After analyzing some expert's comments, you may even reconsider your idea—whether you should proceed with full force, or change into something else. Rather than getting criticism from the loved ones and friends, who may not have relevant experience, I would encourage you to get opinions from experts. Your business communication skills also improve when you are discussing in small, selected groups.

There is a proverb my dad used to say: "Tell me your company; I will tell who you are." The same ideology is applicable to your network as well. Your network is your net worth. Even you may not have a bright business idea yet, but you have the energy to start one. By getting involved in network events, you will get tremendous opportunities. Entrepreneurs like energetic and like-minded people. You may have the potential to participate in new business opportunities, or even get an idea from others. Many people procrastinate with great ideas and, when they find you, with the right energy, they may even want you to be a part of it. I had a great idea to start my own technology company, to provide solutions in the real estate field, for the past two years; but due to various other priorities, I was procrastinating.

While I was coming back from New York City, after attending a seminar last year, I got energized and felt guilty for not proceeding with my idea. Within a few days, I wrote my business plan, but I put off documenting the technical matters due to some other obstacles. Again, this summer, I took my nephews and niece to New York City for a trip, and then realized the mistake I had made again, to not proceed with my great idea. Finally, I wrote the technical information, and approached my software friends and contacts to get their opinion. They were very impressed and wanted to be part of it. Now, my company is in full force, and my main focus is getting the product to the public and making it big in the coming year. Don't be shy; get out there, meet new people, and learn something new.

Mingle with Like-Minded People to Come Out of the Sameness

As I discussed before, you have to do something different from the ordinary, in order to come out of the sameness. When you are connected with people who have the same interests as you, there is no interruption in your mindset when you are alone or with them. While you are with them, you are powered up and more energized. The potential for your growth is exponential. Your positive decision would be wiser, and the criticism you get would also be very true from the experience they have acquired. When you have questions, this circle of friends would have the appropriate answers for you. In order for you to apply within your projects directly, there will be higher potential for new ideas during the brainstorming meetings and discussions. It is same thing if you associate with bad people: you will be influenced by them. I am only talking about associating with the right-minded people to nurture your ideas. Most of the time, your family and long- term friends may not think about your success, and will resist to accept the new adventurous path you are stepping into. They may feel that advising you to stay in the comfort zone, which you are already in, could be the wisest thing, as we all know it is risk free. They won't understand your ambition to come out of the sameness as they are in.

If you feel you are becoming a black swan within your circle of relatives and friends, accept the fact with pride, and focus on your ambitious target. As long as you respect others as you did before, and not offend others, you will be fine. When you run into difficult times, it would be hard to count on everyone to be supportive of you. It is time for you to understand the reality, and embrace the changes in your life.

Knowledge Is a Wealth No One Can Take Away

Every experience or difficulty you may go through would be an accumulation of real life experience. It is a wealth of knowledge that cannot be taught in class, and it will shape your future decision making. No matter what happens in life, this wealth cannot be stolen or diminished, as long as you are alive. Always, when you go through difficult times, think that you are going to come out of it stronger than before. If you think you are going through a difficult situation because you made bad choices, you will be demotivated. We all make bad decisions, but as long as we learn from them, and don't repeat it, that would be a great lesson learned.

When you partner with others or work with investors, they are counting on your credibility, reputation, and knowledge. If your experience is green as grass, there is nothing much they could count on from you at the beginning. I am not promoting you to make mistakes, but when you run into difficulties, face them with courage, and get appropriate help. When you share your horror stories, the majority of ordinary people would nod their head and say that these are the scary reasons they don't get involved in the adventurous projects you are taking on. It is a positive thing for you. Since they are scared of dealing with the ones you are handling and becoming expert at, they would want to offer their hard earned money to invest with you.

Educating yourself in numerous ways will elevate you from the ordinary, to standout. When you advise others during their difficult times, unlike the monetary, your knowledge grows better and better. I remember, in university, while we were studying, I used to give tutorial sessions on a few subjects to my friends. The subjects in which I was able to teach others, I got much higher marks than the other subjects. Even for unforeseen events, if you become broke, your knowledge and your network will assist you to get back on your feet faster than before.

One thing you have to be careful about, if you have an idea that has potential intellectual property that can be stolen by someone, make sure to sign a Nondisclosure Agreement with the person whom you wanted to discuss it with. At the early stage of any technology company or great unique ideas, if you slack on proceeding, and the other person proceeds after listening to you, that idea now belongs to the other person. Since nothing is there for you to backup that the idea was yours, you may not get credit for it. When you are ready your wealth of knowledge could be shared with everyone.

Hire or Follow a Mentor

As we discussed earlier, learning from your own mistakes, and educating yourself, is a great thing. If you wanted to reach your goal even faster, you could learn from others' mistakes. By doing this, your damages are limited, and the loss of time is very minimal as well. Some of the mentors could be expensive to have in the early stages while your financial capabilities are limited. These days, a lot of resources are available via the Internet. You could read about them and learn how they would execute if they were you. You could also learn how they have achieved their success, and the decisions they made, from the start till the success. If you are lucky enough to pay a mentor in the area of expertise you want to thrive in, you will be guided properly to sail your adventurous business through the wave of obstacles. Since you just switched from following instructions to being giving instructions, and sharing your own vision, it is always good to be rechecked by an unbiased expert to make appropriate improvements. Your employees may feel they may offend you by challenging your vision, but your mentor may feel that it is his or her duty. Periodic communication with your mentor would keep you focused on your set goals. It will also help you be accountable to be questioned and give proper guidance.

At the appropriate time, having good mentors will accelerate your thinking process. You could learn a lot from their past experience, and avoid the pitfalls. Even when you run into obstacles, having an expert beside you would give you extra strength. When you are above ordinary people, the difficulties you may face could be unheard of by your circle of friends and relatives. An experienced person could guide you safely, with less damage to you and your business. Now, in the next chapter, let's discuss your loved ones being your bottleneck. It is an interesting chapter in which you can learn a lot.

Chapter 9

Loved Ones Being the Obstacle

They Don't Have the Vision You Have

I remember when I bought my first investment property in Toronto, while I was living in Ottawa. Almost all the people I was associating with at the time, including the realtor who assisted me in buying the property, thought it was a bad investment. The property was in very bad shape. The dishwasher smelled bad. The weeds in the lawn had grown to more than a foot high. The carpet in the basement was stained and smelled bad. On the first day of my new purchase, my wife stepped into the house, and then she got out of it immediately, due to the unbearable condition in which the house was kept. To my eye, it was a great opportunity. The property's lot size for the location was great. The location was in an upcoming, upscale neighborhood, in the year 2009. The subway line was just minutes away, and the main bus route was just two blocks away. I knew, with a few thousand dollars, I could get most of it restored for a rental property.

I took a few days off work, and brought in additional help and a handyman to tidy and repair all the necessary issues. Once everything was taken care of, thankfully, I was able to rent it for a positive cash flow. In the past several years, the appreciation in the neighborhood has skyrocketed, and the value has gone up drastically. Most of the houses in the neighbourhood got demolished and turned into multimillion dollar homes, while my little duckling stayed within the very large, custom-made houses, in one of the prestigious neighborhoods in Canada. Even in the coming years, it has only an upside. Everyone looked at the condition of the property at the time, while I was picturing what I was going to turn that into. In my eyes, I only saw the property I have converted it into, rather than the immediate look of it.

When you buy a small business, if the sale is low, and if you have a great plan to push the sale higher, and increase the profit, you should go for it. Not everyone visualizes the opportunities with a great vision. While most ordinary people run away from the badly performing business or real estate, the visionary entrepreneur, like you, comes in and takes things into your own hands, to turn that into a profitable business. It enables you to get a bigger dividend than by buying a profitable business. When you acquire a successful business, or well-kept real estate, there is nothing much you can do to improve the sales in the business, or to force the property's appreciation.

When you have a great idea to start your own business, you have to have a great vision for a successful path. People around you may advise conservatively. If you start to listen to everyone who cares about you, you will be bombarded with guidance, in multiple directions. You could get the financial and moral support from your immediate family and long-term friends, but don't let them influence your passion. If you fail to have your own strong vision, then your business would be a ship that starts to sail without a captain. When you are determined and have a short and long-term goal, you will pave a path for your success. Even if the whole world is against you, don't give up. Your relatives and friends cannot envision your vision.

They Think They Are Protecting You, but are Actually Limiting Your Capability

It starts from childhood: when a child is good in art or sports, the parents may promote, or even divert, the child to study math and science. The parents may think, if their child becomes a doctor, lawyer, accountant, or an engineer, that they will have a successful career and a reasonable lifestyle. When someone is diverted from what they are good at, and are passionate about, their motivation level goes down. The pleasure they get from what they do, lacks. The creativity would dwindle. As long as the child is not drifting onto the wrong path, the parents should let them try and flourish in what they love doing.

I remember, when I started my real estate investments, my parents and siblings would tell me that I am in engineering, and dealing with the tenants would be an unnecessary headache. With a young family, it would be stressful to me. I do not have a history of real estate investing knowledge in the family either. Their thought was that I had a well-paying job and a young family. If I worked till the age of 65, I could have adequate savings and a peaceful retirement. No one knew I was fast tracking to come out of the employee status at the age of 42, instead of 65. Keep your curiosity high. We will discuss this in detail, later in the chapters. In my case, I was an out of town investor, and it required a lot of travelling at the beginning. We never sat down and discussed pros and cons about real estate investment. I would say you should listen to everyone, and don't offend them by shutting them down. In case you run into financial difficulties, or need moral support, some of them will be there for you.

The protectionism, without proper analytical thought, is not useful. Your family and your friends would look at you in a similar way to themselves. They somehow want to keep you in the sameness as they are in. You should be able to fly like a butterfly, rather than sit longer inside the cocoon, like a caterpillar. The creative opportunities are endless for an entrepreneur like you, while the jobs are limited for employees who depend on someone like you.

No Knowledge in the Field They Were Advising

In most cases, the relatives and friends who try to advise may not have the relevant experience for what they are trying to talk to you about. I was talking with my 12-year- old son the other day, and I asked him, "Would you ask your French teacher about your doubts in Math?" Without any hesitation, he responded, "No, Dad, you should ask the Math teacher about any doubts in Math, and vice versa." Wow, it is the same philosophical thought applicable to getting advice in your entrepreneurship. It is not their fault that they do not have the relevant knowledge, but they try their best to influence you. Unless the person has the relevant experience on the subject they are talking about, let the advice go in one ear and out the other, and don't process it. If you are married and wanted to start up something new, do not ask your husband or wife for advice, but convince them to be supportive of your new journey you are about to embark upon. I know your other half, or parents, would hate me when they hear this. It is the practical reality. In Robert Kiyosaki's Rich Dad Poor Dad book, he wasn't praising or teaching about his own dad's lifestyle. He learned business knowledge from his friend's dad, who was a businessman. You have to make appropriate corrections in your way of living to achieve something meaningful.

Unless your parent is an entrepreneur, it would be hard for a typical employee parent to advise an energetic visionary person like you. You could be a growing teenager, or a new immigrant, or someone wanting to reach your dream—don't let your loved ones be your bottleneck. If you allow that to happen, you will regret it in the later stages of your life. The people who do not take risks are the people who are taking a big risk by counting on someone to take care of them. Thinking like 99% of people will not get you the success you have been craving. I want you to have a backup plan while you get into the new territory of entrepreneurship. Let's discuss the details in the next chapter.

Chapter 10

Acquire Fixed Assets and Adventure Business Opportunities

Accumulate Income-Producing Assets

While you have the income through your employment, you should start accumulating income-producing assets. It depends on the city you are living in, but in most of the major cities around the world, real estate is quite expensive. What we think of as expensive today, could be cheaper twenty years from now. You don't need to buy a million dollar piece of real estate to start with. If your capital is limited, start buying smaller properties within town, or even out of town. At this point, even if you have to pay a few hundred dollars to cover the monthly expenses from your own pocket, I would encourage you to go for it. Right now you have your employment income to cover the little shortfall. The best scenario is getting positive cash flow properties, but if the city you are living in is extremely expensive, and only allows yourself to go for this type of negative cash flow property, for the long term, it would still be more highly beneficial than not acquiring it.

Don't exceed your negative cash flow properties to more than a couple. Repeat your purchasing process till all the major banks deny lending you due to the maximum lending capacity for individuals or corporations. Within this portfolio of properties, you could have single houses, townhouses, duplexes, triplexes, or even four plexes. Don't jump into commercial yet. Learn every aspect of managing the rental properties. You may have chances of running into issues and solving them. This is the best way to learn and harden your experience.

Once the bank starts to hesitate on the residential side, and you now have the hang of handling rental properties, get into commercial apartment buildings and office or business space. Some people may advise to get into commercial right away, but I would like you to learn and make sure you can handle this new experience. I can guarantee this is not for everyone. It has exponential financial growth, but it is a painful process too. For commercial real estate, the major banks, especially in North America, don't lend based on your income capability; it is based on the real estate balance sheet. If that particular real estate building is producing a positive cash flow, and you or your company has good credit with a good reputation, you will have higher chances of getting financed, with the required down payment and the closing costs from you. Another reason I like you to have a portfolio of residential assets is because it can be cashed in within a reasonable amount of time, compared to the commercial real estate. If your property already has quite a bit of equity, and you need the money urgently, by reducing the sale price, you could attract many prospective buyers. In the commercial world, the buyers are investors like you, and want to acquire at a discounted price. The commercial buyers are also a very small percentage compared to the residential home buyers.

You may wonder where I get the money to invest in all these properties. It does not happen overnight, unlike what has happened to the social media company founders these days. Even for them, it took several years, but they reached billions of dollars in net worth much faster. As the years go by, your property is getting paid off by your tenant, and the property is appreciating. Now, with the rental income and your employment income, you could try to get a second position loan from the banks, as a secured line of credit, for a low interest rate. In Canada, you could get it for prime plus 0.5% or 1%. It all depends on your credit rating. It used to be even just the prime rate.

You may think of one or two profit centres when owning a real estate holding, but the following are the major benefits of the real estate holdings I see:

1) Potential to purchase at discounted price
2) Tenant pays down your mortgage
3) Long-term appreciation
4) Forced appreciation
5) Ability to own and benefit from a 100% value of an asset, while investing probably 22% of the value of an asset

Do not worry about all the negativity others may discuss or bring to you. Now you are prepared and getting into action. Go with full force, and become a savvy investor and business operator. If you want to learn more details about the five profit centres I have discussed above, you may want to visit **www.fireyourjobbook.com.**

Accumulate Liquid Assets

While you accumulate fixed assets, you should start to accumulate emergency funds too. If you are still an employee, many corporations have a certain percentage as employer matching for the retirement funds you contribute via the company. You should capitalize this great opportunity to maximize your liquid savings. When you contribute to a registered retirement plan, the government will also give you the tax break for the amount you invest in. This is the case in Canada and the US. In Canada, the retirement savings is called RRSP, and in the US, it is called 401K. In Canada, we have the Tax Free Savings Account as well. There is a limit set by the government each year, and it can be accumulated. If you are still a student, or newly self-employed, it may not be applicable. It is always good to know beforehand.

I would strongly discourage you from saving money in the bank, and keeping it in the account as cash. The cash value goes down as the years pass, due to inflation. You could talk to your banker, and park it in secured funds, where at least you will beat the inflation with very little risk. Even if you are young, don't take a high risk on this while your major investment is in real estate holdings. When the financial market goes down, everything goes down. These days, the world has become too small and well connected. It does not matter if you have invested in real estate, gold, or stocks. During the last financial crisis, from 2007 to 2009, in the US, none of the asset classes escaped. During this time, Canada escaped with a mild recession that was short-lived. It did not matter if you had invested in Europe, Australia, or North America, and diversified your investment into multiple sectors; unfortunately, all went into the negative territory. The secondary way I practice growing liquid assets is to become a bank, and do secured lending to reputable people who have real estate projects or holdings. You could easily get a 10% to 15% return on investment by doing it. All these are avenues to participate in various projects, and to learn the potentials out there while you are paving a path for your financial independence.

Don't Be Afraid to Start and Fail Start-up Businesses

While you are at your full-time paying job, during your spare time, try new venturous projects in real estate, small businesses, or even ambitious high tech start-ups, which would enable you to get the feel of whether you really want to seriously proceed with that particular dream, or if it is time to change. While you make the changes or optimize your thoughts, you still have your full-time paying job to fall back on. The only thing you have to lose is your spare TV or sports time, and in some cases, money. Still, when you seriously go through the cycle of experimenting with your business idea, you would have learned a lot. If you are a student, there is time to experiment, fail, and learn now rather than later. Instead of not trying it while you are working, if you have experimented, failed, and finalized your targeted business, you will be way ahead in your game of success.

I tried investing in stocks right after graduating from university, and lost thousands of dollars. I also explored a few business opportunities at the feasibility study level, before I started investing in real estate. I even discussed with a few business people about importing and exporting goods as well. One time, I researched and looked for a location for a grocery store in Toronto, while I was working in Ottawa as an engineer.

All the losses and the time spent on those studies were well worth it. Those made me stronger than before, and my purpose became stronger and stronger, as I did not gain something tangible from my efforts. Sometimes it is like the kids—when you deny them something, they really want to have it. If you offer it to them all the time, they are no longer interested.

Even though I agree that it is never too late to try, any failure impacts at a young age is more easily managed than later in your life. It could be that your financial capability at that age is less, and your loss would be minimal. You also have high energy and motivation when you are younger, compared to after your fifties. Your responsibilities are less at a young age and, even if you run into financial difficulties, it can be manageable. When you have a family with kids, a mortgage, and bills, it would be hard to take any financial risk, and the failure impacts may even jeopardise your marriage.

Don't Widen Your Industry at the Beginning

While you are trying out projects, it is better to stick within similar fields rather than random industries. For an example, when you invest in real estate, you could have a property management company or an investment company, or even a development company. All these multiple, relevant businesses will educate you, and make you more knowledgeable in the industry in which you are experimenting to grow. In one of these businesses, for an example, if you start to see success and potential organic growth, you could repeat the process. I would encourage you to develop your own system, in whatever business in which you are seeing the light at the end of the tunnel. Once you have the system and the repeatable successes, you could repeat what you have already done. If things need to be documented, and you want to make sure you have a proven system, spend some time and recheck if your system is bullet proof. When you document your system as a procedure, it allows you to identify where the holes are, and the ways to fix them. At the beginning, aimlessly going after various industries may make you less of an expert, and it would be hard to repeat your success. You don't want to reinvent the wheel, over and over again.

Never Shy Away From Bringing Partners or Investors on Board

An entrepreneur requires more distinguished qualities than an employee. Even if you lack a few, you could always partner with someone who could be a complement to your expertise. If you wait to develop all the traits yourself, time and the industry evolution is not going to wait for you. Apple INC. would not have developed their computers, and wouldn't have become famous, if Steve Jobs waited to know how to build the computers by himself. He partnered with the tech-savvy Steve Wozniak; with Steve Jobs' remarkable vision, he developed the business, and the rest is history. If you want to open small businesses, there are numerous opportunities. While you have your full- time job, you could become a money partner with an existing business owner, and get involved in the management side, or partner with an industry expert, and create a new one. You could take on the business development and management side, while the industry expert takes on the day to day operations. You have already adopted lot of changes in your lifestyle while reading through the past chapters, and now it is time to get into the action and flourish.

Start-up businesses sometimes fail or dwindle due to insufficient funding. If you are acquiring properties, or starting up business, you could always bring in investment partners to have sufficient funding to take off and grow. With limited capital, the growth would be minimal. By giving away a portion of the equity in your company, at the early stage, you could bring in employees for lower than the market salary, as well as advisers and investors. It's all in how you think: you either want to have one hundred percent of a small pie, or a certain percentage of a bigger pie. The following graphs show the visual representation:

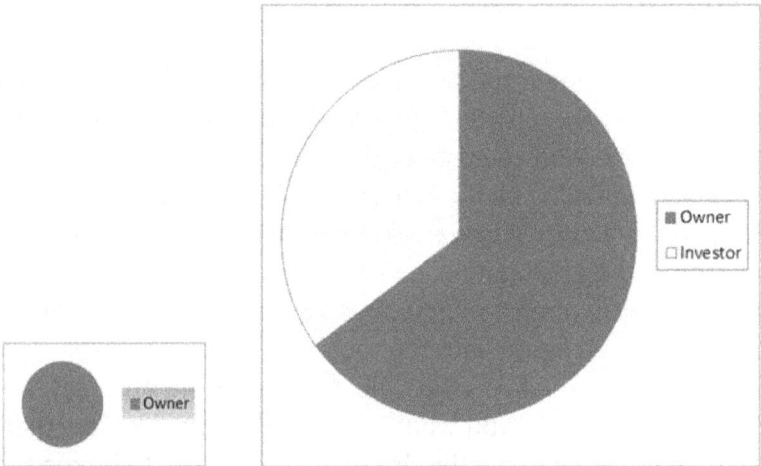

When you bring savvy investors on board, they will be your catalyst to grow faster, and to succeed in your endeavor. Now that you have your business up and running, let's discuss the potential ways to get assistance and grow your business, while not stepping into someone else's shoes.

Chapter 11

Don't Mix Business with Relationships

Have a Clear Understanding of Responsibilities, Compensation, and Exit Strategies

When you are starting a small business, having a plan of how things will be executed, and what the responsibilities of the business partners will be, is crucial. If you have a business partner, make sure your expectation is understood by that individual, and he or she is accountable for delivering it. If you are the industry expert, and your partner has the knowledge in accounting and bookkeeping, let them handle the accounts payable, accounts receivable, keeping the books in order, and dealing with the corporate accountant. When the responsibilities are not discussed before getting together as business partners, and when you identify the mismatch, it would be tough to replace the partner who has already officially joined your passionate business. Take your time to discuss with potential people; then, once the assurance is received, you could take them on as your business partners. I met an energetic lady who had started her own passionate business. While she was raising capital, she got investment from an expert, and he became the BOD member of the company. Unfortunately, he became a headache for her; he wasn't cooperative with her decisions. When I met her, she was so frustrated, and was trying to find ways to buy him out and get rid of him. Unfortunately, I was able to sense that this particular issue was bringing her energy down, and not helping the business.

Business partners or employees may join for various reasons. They may say they are excited about the business or the technology, and may not discuss the compensation at the beginning. Most people don't take things very seriously at the beginning. It is better to stipulate the monetary compensation, or the equity split, sooner than later. As the business grows, and multiple people start to join, things get complicated when things are not defined properly. If your business fails, no one cares. When your business becomes successful, everyone wants a piece of the pie. The latecomers, who identified the growth, may wish to get credit for the sweat that was contributed by the early partners and you.

Any business you explore should have an exit strategy. Even though you love your idea, and it is your passion, do not tie yourself emotionally to the business. Within a certain timeline, your business should be tested in the market to see the potential growth. You should have a business plan to turn your business into a profitable one as well. You don't want to continually work and pay for your passionate business loss. Your business should be treated as a separate entity, with you being the executer, along with others. Even with your business partners, you could also have an exit strategy: if the business does not meet their ambitious target, they could exit at a certain stage. Your timeline of the exit could be longer, and you might be able to withstand the loss for a longer time than the others. You do not want to legally keep an unwilling partner in your business, for longer than they desire. It will not help the business or bring positive energy to the table.

Don't Take Things for Granted

At the beginning, when you start your business, an easy and fast way to get help is through your close friends and relatives. Even with them, from the beginning, and when things become serious, make sure to stipulate the compensation they will receive. For an example, if your brother or friend takes care of the marketing side of the business, you could give them a position within your organization, and compensate them with equity or monetary funds. It will motivate them to continue to work with you, and dedicate more time for you. If you think it is for free, and continue to expect this, they may be inclined to help you for a while, but then they may prioritize your tasks as low, compared to many of their other activities. I wouldn't be surprised if they totally declined to help you, down the road. You won't be in a position to demand assistance or ask them to be accountable either.

I remember one of my friends who had good educated business management and practical knowledge of running a business. He had started a small business, and it was running profitable at the beginning. When he wanted to grow the business, he reached out to his own siblings and friends to raise the investment funds. He had used that fund for his own business growth, while the money lenders were not given any equity position or any profit sharing mechanism. The money was given as per his credibility, and the other people wanted him to be successful in his business. During the expansion of his business, things did not work as he had originally planned, and he encountered a huge loss. He could not even return the capital he had borrowed from others. His credibility was lost, and he went through a very difficult financial situation where he could not even count on moral support from his close circle of family and friends. If he would have brought them in as equity partners, or a predefined profit sharing scheme, after illustrating the risk and the benefit of the business they were about to invest in, he would have had to share the profit or loss. Even the loss he encountered would have been shared by multiple people. In this case, he wanted to keep one hundred percent of the profit to himself, and he did not think the business might encounter loss. It is better not to take others' time, effort, and monetary contribution for free. When you share your growth, and keep them as part of it, people want to participate more, and they will go beyond their means to be supportive of you.

Don't Cross the Line

When you try to attract investments for your company, you have to let people understand your business, and make their appropriate decision. If their goal in partnering with your business does not synchronize with your objective, it does not matter how much money they want to invest with you. You should not proceed with that transaction. You don't want to show the potential investor you are in need or that you are desperate. When you are desperate, you will be in a weaker position to negotiate, and will have to accept the terms and conditions of the investor, which may not be favourable for you.

If you are a student and trying to put together a business, you cannot just bring in your party friends to start a business.

You have to make sure the individuals, whom you will be taking on as your business partners, will bring in some expertise that would be beneficial for the company. In some instances, people may have very good expertise, and want to be part of the business, but they do not have the willingness to contribute their time. Similarly, if someone has no knowledge, these individuals may not be suitable to bring in as active business partners. When you identify a mismatch, don't proceed with them. Unwilling partners can be more troublesome than useful to the team. When you identify the right people, make sure they appreciate your idea and understand the high potential. In some cases, when they understand it clearly, they may give you more good ideas to enhance your business. You should be dynamic enough to accept all the good ideas, rather than exclusively relying on your original plan. Make sure they are reasonably committed to contribute to your business needs. I would encourage you not to bring in business partners who do not appreciate your idea, or are not willing to commit their time and effort.

As I said earlier, as an entrepreneur, you should prepare yourself to add team members, and be able to hire experts as required. At the same time, you should be in a position to get rid of the mismatched team members, or business partners, in a professional way. Your business is like your baby and it needs a lot of direction at the beginning, while solely relying on you.

When you deal with customers or tenants, you have to respect them and make sure you are serving them to satisfy their needs. Even when you encounter a creepy customer, you have to treat them equally. When you deal with tenants, you have to be especially careful in dealing with them. Some professional tenants would dig multiple holes, till you fall in to one of them.

For an example, if a tenant is being too nice to you, and is being friendly with you, and then they start to complain about multiple things, you should not ignore their complaints. Things should be documented and, after making sure the issues are legitimate, you should get them fixed. Some tenants would complain via email, and then verbally offer to do it themselves. You should take this as your own business responsibility, and handle it, and thank them for what they have offered. Don't ever let your ego show while dealing with your tenants, customers, or even your business partners. If you express anything emotionally or unprofessionally, it will cause damage to you and your business in the long term.

People Watch and Will Approach You

When you start your early business, people may think you will fail, or even that it is a waste of time. At the early stage, when you approach them for investment, or even ask them to associate with you on your business activities, some of them may deny this too. You should not give up when you encounter issues like these. After you work hard and become successful, people will see the potential in you and in your business. When you bring in repeated success, you will see an influx of interest to associate with you or invest with you. I was training in Taekwondo, and we do most of the exercise sequences in three repetitions. As we do the third one, our muscles get tired, and some of us may give up. Our training master told us, when you do it the first time, it is a fluke. The second time, it shows some degree of effort. When you do it the third time, you have a definite purpose in your action. With definite purpose, you can achieve the set goals you aim for.

It is like how a dead tree does not attract birds, animals, or even humans, while the large, growing tree would attract numerous living things, for various purposes. When your business grows successfully, many people will have an appetite to join and invest with you. You should be able to carefully weed out the unmatched ones, and collaborate with the matched individuals to mature your business. While you are putting in effort to bring up a successful business and having a full time job, it is not easy. Even though you are paving a path for your success to be financially independent, you are not there yet. Let's discuss how to handle the situation professionally. I am proud of you for getting to this stage with me, and for learning a lot to achieve your financial freedom.

Chapter 12

Keep the Professionalism at High Priority

Only Share Your Thoughts and Ventures with Like-Minded Colleagues

While you are successfully bringing up your passionate business, you might also have many things going on at your demanding full-time job. Occasionally, you may feel tempted to share your ideas and success with your colleagues during your coffee break, or while having a casual discussion. It all depends on the individual with whom you intend to share your thoughts. Narrow-minded people may get offended when you share your hardworking personal success with them, while you are still working full-time. They may feel left out, or that it is something that they did not achieve. They wouldn't hesitate to bring you down with any kind of negativity about your business, and they would even go beyond to stab you in the back by finding fault in your work and your commitment. When they try to give you a hard time in the work environment, it would be an unnecessary stress for you. I find prematurely sharing your business potentials at your work place, with the wrong people, while you have not achieved anything tangible in your own business, will not help you at all. Keeping a very low profile, and sharing with the right individuals, would assist your business prosperity.

While you are starting your own business, first make sure there is no conflict of interest with the current job you have. If you are a student or are self-employed, most likely you will have no issues in doing any kind of business. If you start a business that is a similar industry and is potential competition to the current employer, that may raise a conflict of interest and a legal issue. Make sure you are not violating the company policies while you are trying to create something on your own.

Sometimes you may identify like-minded individuals; they may have the same passion as you, and the expertise they pose that could be essential for your business. As per your working relationship, if you identify someone as an individual who you could trust, then invite them to have a detailed business discussion outside of the work place, to see if they are interested in your idea. You could ask them to keep the discussion private till you are ready to share with others. There could be a potential for someone to be a money partner, or to be involved as an active partner, to participate in your business operations and development. You cannot leave any doors closed, but at the same time, you have to be cautious enough about how you are handling it.

Make Sure Not to Let Down Your Current Employer

Now, you are quite busy with your own projects, and need to handle multiple things while finishing the tasks at work, or putting in the required number of working hours you have been assigned. If you are a student or are self-employed, you might feel the same pressure to multi-task, and will lose your entertainment and Friday night hanging out with your buddies. Instead, now you can adopt a new lifestyle, of meeting new people and having business meetings.

This is the phase in your business stage where you have to be very careful not to be unproductive at work, which pays your bills at this time. I totally agree it is a painful stage, when you see the bright future ahead of you, and a lot needs to be done. Now, you may not be as motivated as you were a few years ago to take on challenging new tasks at work and put in extra hours. If the time doesn't permit, don't go beyond to put in extra hours or work overtime. It is for your utmost benefit that you make sure you are putting better effort than before to get things done at work. When I am motivated and energized, I can do a lot of things. I trust you could do it too. I have done that in my transition period. You should not have any excuses not to be productive at work. It is a very good example that you have to show: when people count on you, you take extra steps to deliver what is expected of you, or you even surpass this. Your right-minded colleagues, managers, or your employer could be your future potential business partners, or they could even introduce you to the right people.

Negotiate to Get a Pay Cut if Needed

Now, your new start-up business begins to make some revenue, and is producing net profit, rather than you and your business partners pumping in your own money to run the business. If you are in need of more time to dedicate towards your own business, while you still have your full-time employment, now is the time to slowly break your silence.

Whatever you did not share before, does not matter. Since you sacrificed your own leisure time in pursuit of your own projects, it wasn't deliberately hidden information. Hence, it was a personal matter, and you don't need to advertise to everyone unnecessarily.

Do not disappear, or call in sick often from your work, to take care of your own business during business hours. You will lose your credibility and reputation by doing this. While I was working as an engineering consultant, I was working five days per week, and eight hours per day at Ericsson. Since my real estate business was growing, and I had to deal with multiple people during business hours, I desperately needed some allocated time. I was hesitant to make this move, but I had no choice at the time, and I was glad I made the move, which I am promoting to many people nowadays. I set up a meeting with the manager, with whom I was providing my services, and explained to him my situation of needing to reduce my consulting service time. Even though I was working flexible hours, I told him I did not want to take off and sometimes not be able to attend the meetings during work hours, to attend my own business meetings. He appreciated my honesty, and asked me about my business to make sure there was no conflict of interest. Since he needed my services, and wanted me to continue without any interruption, he suggested that I work an extra hour each day, and offered for me to take every Friday afternoon off. Instead of asking for a salary raise, I was asking for a pay cut, but I got my valuable time from having at least a half working day off, every week, while not reducing my consulting income.

I still remember how one of my colleagues, who used to be a very good friend of mine, became agitated about my arrangement with the management. He even complained directly to me that I should not do that, and that it may bring down my productivity to the company for which I was providing the services. Even though it was none of his business, he pretended he was the dedicated company man, and tried to question me. There are times when you have to ignore people like these, and move on with your own set of goals, while not jeopardising your professionalism. In this case, I had to ignore that individual, and carry on with my tasks. I am glad to identify those people early, and not disclose any details about my business to them. When you identify people like these, do not worry about it, and don't feel bad about losing colleagues or friends. It is better to lose them than keep the illegitimate people who are portrayed as good friends. You should be very pleased that you are able to identify the real side of people at certain times.

I stopped my consultancy and became a permanent employee at Syntronic Canada. Within six months, I had communicated with my new management, and negotiated to get a pay cut in order to get every Friday off. People work so hard and negotiate to get a pay increase, but I negotiated to get a pay cut in order to gain 20% of my working hours, in a week, to be dedicated to my business. I will tell you the eventual outcome after a year. One of my contractor friends works full-time and does home repairs and renovations part-time. I give him business quite often on my properties in the Greater Toronto Area. A couple of months ago, he complained to me that he was getting lots of contracts through referrals; but, unfortunately, he had to turn most of them away due to his full-time job. He was concerned about losing the medical coverage he was getting though the company insurance, and didn't want to lose his full-time job. After chatting with him, I asked him if he had good reputation within the company he works. He said they assign him overtime and extended hours because he was one of the good employees at work. In this case, I told him to be confident and set up an appointment with his direct manager or human resource person, and ask for a pay cut, and offer to take a nonpaid day off, each week, when the company is not extremely busy. It turned out that his company was usually slow on Mondays. They granted his wish of a pay cut, and now, every Monday, he has off as a long weekend. When you are confident and honest about your intentions, people will respect you. The worst thing that could happen is they may deny your request. If they deny your genuine request, it is too bad, but now your purpose becomes stronger, and now you are fired up more than ever. The latest motivation will accelerate you to reach your final goal much sooner than later.

Integrity at Stake

Even when you know you are not going to be at your workplace long enough to benefit from the bonuses or salary raises, it is good to keep the caliper of your energy high till the end. It will prove how committed and reputable you are. I remember, just nine months prior, I had chosen to become a nonemployee; I was assigned a new task to design and deliver a complete working product. I was one of the lead designers for the design solution. Due to the customer's request, the schedule was very tight. Even though I was supposed to take every Friday off, and that summer I had to sell a couple of assets in Ottawa to make my final move, I offered to work nights, Fridays, and on the weekends, for the success of the project. We had customers coming from Japan for a demonstration, and I worked with them to explain the functionality, and demonstrated in the lab. When we had issues during the system testing, I was there, optimizing and fixing the system. I would work later at night and on the weekends to take care of my own real estate portfolios, and make major decisions for my ground-breaking changes in my life. It was very tiring and painful, but I had to do what I was enlightened to do. If you are determined, anything can happen. If there is no will power, nothing can be achieved.

Many people, when they start to focus on their own business and see the success, they may start to overreact to that success, and they forget that the present bills are still getting paid by the current employer. Your years of reputation cannot be destroyed in your last 12 or 6 months of employment period. More patience and courage is required during the transition period. Instead of jumping the gun and completely walking out of your job, if possible, take a pay cut, and extend your day job to make sure your business is growing with strong roots. It is always easier to extend your stay as an employee rather than fully come out of it and then try to go back. It will create unnecessary negative energy and a bad reputation. You have been a very determined person, and you have assets and an operating business to back you up. Let's discuss how you could start to smell the financial freedom.

Chapter 13

Generate Passive Income and Start Building Your Business

Start Consolidating Investments and Income Potentials

If you need to create a passive or active income while growing your new adventurous business, there are many ways you could generate this. For an example, if you are a professional, and an expert on what you do, you could allocate some time for consulting, while you spend most of your time on developing your new business. At the same time, as advised in an earlier chapter, you should have some liquid cash funds available on standby, which can support your new unexpected business losses, as well as look after you and your family financially when you are not receiving biweekly pay cheques. If your spouse has a job that would bring income to the table, that is a bonus too. Another backup plan is to have passive income-producing investments. You should have invested in an active business that is operated by the active business partner, while sharing the profit or real estate income-producing properties. If you don't have full- time employment, and are in need of money desperately, it would be very difficult to obtain it. The potential lenders would look at you as a high risk, and wouldn't want to jeopardise their funds while you are experimenting with your idea, without an income. People would start injecting their money as soon as you start to produce credible, positive results, and can stand out with the concept of a valuable business.

I would encourage you to consolidate your income-producing properties to maximize the monthly net operating income. If you still own a couple of properties, and those need your monthly injection of funds, it is time for you to force the appreciation by remodeling or renovating, and selling them. You should use the funds from the sale proceeds to pay off your other outstanding debts or loans on the positive cash flowing properties. It will increase your monthly cash flow for the bright future you desire. Some people prematurely start to use the money, and buy expensive cars to treat themselves, or even buy a bigger house to show off their wealth. I would strongly recommend you refrain from doing that, and stick with the plan and your purpose. If you want to be very conservative and firm enough to be financially headache free, you should have accumulated at least eight income-producing properties by now. If you have a few apartment buildings, and an income-producing business already, that would be great.

Let's discuss in detail why I like having at least eight income-producing properties, purchased mainly for income rather than for betting on the appreciation only. In Ontario, Canada, where I live now in 2017, you could purchase a residential property in the range of $200 000 to $250 000, and rent it for $1600 per month. If you had started to accumulate properties six to eight years ago, the average purchase price could have been less than

$200 000 per property. Let's do the following calculation conservatively. I want you do the proper due diligence while you make your own decision in your geographic area. One thing I want you to be aware of, I am not talking about purchasing properties in Toronto now, but I have even acquired single homes in the Greater Toronto Area, for $211 000, five years ago. Those days are long gone now. Let's do the detailed math, analytically. The following is a sample scenario calculation for you to enlighten your brain.

Assumption:

- Tenant pays utilities, and maintains the property by cutting the grass in the summer and shoveling snow in the winter. It is the beauty of the residential properties. You could legally pass along some of your responsibilities to the tenant.

- Outstanding mortgage on each property = $150 000

- Current interest rate for 5 years fixed = 2.8%

- Mortgage amortization period = 25 years

- Average property tax for each property per annum = $2500

- Number of properties you have accumulated = 08

- None of the income properties are condos, so no condo fees

- Let's assume your property is in great shape and has a zero vacancy rate.

Since we are being very conservative, the properties are only rented to single families, and not rented to two families or student housing to maximize the rental income.

Potential Expense:

- Monthly mortgage payment on each property per month = ~ $710

- Monthly property Insurance = ~ $70

- Monthly property tax payment = $2500/12 = $208.33

- Allocated monthly maintenance expense per month = $150

- Total monthly expense per property = $1138.33

Potential Conservative Income:

- Monthly income per property = $1600

- Monthly projected net income = 1600*8 − 1138.33*8 = $12800 − $9106.64 = $3693.36

- Annual net income = $44320.32

Roughly $44000 per annum income can support a middle class family, even with a small mortgage loan, while you expand your venturous project that has proven to have an enormous potential. I will tell you the secret happening in the above properties. From the monthly mortgage payment you are paying on each property, within five years, roughly $21 788 of capital is getting paid off. Can you imagine the total capital gets paid off on all eight properties within five years? The astronomical amount is $174 304. As the capital gets paid off by your tenants, your monthly positive cash flow is going to increase. I could have suggested that you sell three properties, and pay off the debt on the other five properties as much as you could, to increase the monthly cash flow, but I want you to get the maximum benefit through owning multiple properties for the long term. By owning more assets, your mortgage is getting paid off on multiple properties, and it will increase your net positive cash flow down the road. You could also accumulate the equity through the appreciation as well. It is a great example for you to understand that you don't need to have million dollar properties in your portfolio to find your financial independence.

In 2008, I set my goal to acquire investment properties. Prior to those years, I had personal experience through the property I was living in, and my brother's property, which were appreciating for quite some time. While I was seriously researching the location and visiting the properties to purchase in the Greater Toronto Area and Ottawa, the US was in recession. That is the time when major banks in the US and Europe had a financial crisis. The governments had to bail out those troubled banks, for billions of dollars. With my real estate knowledge being green as grass, I kept on increasing my knowledge, and was looking for discounted deals. At this time, US real estate was melting down. In some states, there was even news about people who were just leaving the keys in their houses, and walking away due to not being able to pay the mortgage, utilities, and tax bills. It turned out to be, in late 2008, that Canada also officially went into recession.

At that time, I read about the 1988 real estate astronomical appreciation, and then the melt down, in Canada, and especially in Toronto. In early 1990, the real estate melt down lasted for quite some years in the Greater Toronto Area. I was telling myself that house prices were going to go down in Canada as well; potentially, I could wait for few more years to acquire more discounted properties. One great thing I did was to start making offers at a discounted price, which could be worthwhile in six months after depreciation. It was no surprise; I did not get any accepted offers. I was watching the economy activities very closely, and the real estate prices. I will tell you one thing: when you buy properties, don't get into the market and then just purchase something for the sake of purchasing it. If you are in it seriously, and want to be wiser, you had better test the market with low offers, and understand the present market price and the trend before committing yourself. The price depreciation only lasted till spring 2009, and then the real estate prices started to climb. I did miss the bottom price, but I caught it when it was stabilized and rising.

The curve graph on the following page shows how I have studied the real estate trend, and make it work for me.

From the graph, you can clearly see, just before the real estate price hits the bottom at point A, it is tough to predict when the falling knife is going to stop. You should patiently watch the price hit the bottom, and witness the stability and the price pick up. Till you see the price pick up, you will not know the bottom. You may think I am not advising you to purchase it at point A, right at the bottom of the real estate price. It is very hard to predict and take actions in a timely manner right at the bottom. Unlike stock trading, real estate transactions take a

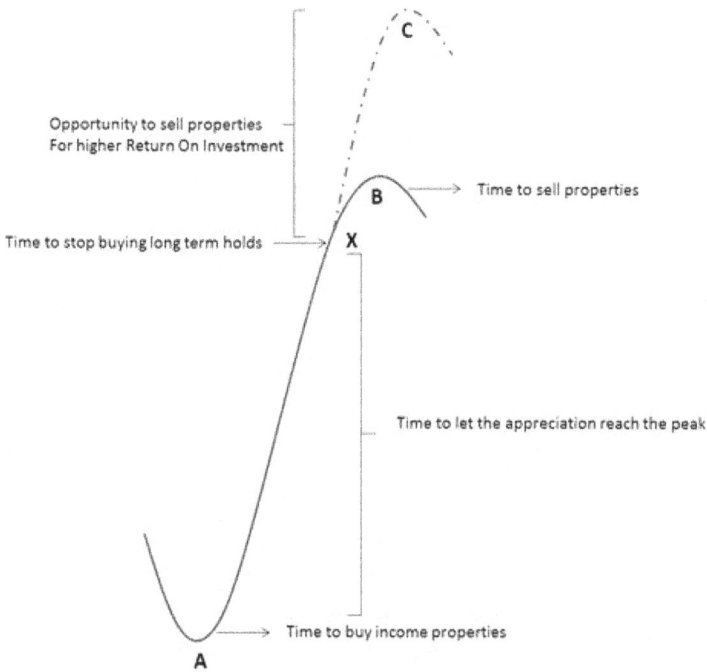

Opportunity to sell properties
For higher Return On Investment

Time to sell properties

Time to stop buying long term holds

Time to let the appreciation reach the peak

Time to buy income properties

longer time. While the price decline takes place till the price increase happens, the bottom price is not known yet. Once the shift occurred, the bottom price became the past. When the appreciation starts to occur, the ride usually takes a longer time until it reaches around the point X. You should enjoy and keep accumulating properties till you witness the point X where everyone is getting into the real estate frenzy, the prices are very high, and the media starts to talk. The government also starts to intervene by placing regulations related to real estate transactions. You should not purchase for long- term holds at this stage of the real estate cycle. This is the phase when everyone is tempted to line up and buy, but you have to be the cautious one. Similar to the bottom price, the highest price point is also hard to predict. Till you witness the price decline, you don't know when the Bull ride is going to end. Until you see the negative shift in price increase, point B could potentially go to point C, and then turn downwards. In this case, just learn to accept the price decline from the peak, and start to cash in right at the down turn. It would be a smarter move to maximize the profit. Otherwise, you would not know the appreciation duration and, without realizing the full potential, you do not want to sell it prematurely.

Redefine Your Purpose and Process

The set goals and the milestones you would have laid out before, may need to be revisited now. It is time to redefine and make sure it aligns with your major purpose. When you were originally starting out and laying your plans, your knowledge and the network of contacts could have been very limited. Now, you came out of your comfort zone, and are making things happen in a positive way. You have learned lot through the years as well.

If you have a mentor, have a detailed discussion with him or her to go through the process and your goals. If any adjustments need to be done, feel free to make the changes. I remember, I had set a goal to reach a million-dollar net worth, ten years ago. Now, that set amount won't give you financial freedom if you are living in the Greater Toronto Area, or in any other big cities. The minimum wage, and real estate prices, along with other essential items, had gone up drastically, well above the inflation rate. If your business already sees exponential growth, that is great for you, and makes your decision very easy. If you would have come through numerous bumpy roads, with lots of setbacks, it would be very difficult. Still, you will be a much stronger and wiser person compared to the others who stayed without taking on any challenging projects you had worked on. In order to achieve your purpose, it should be very creative and it has to be beyond your selfishness. Now, if your purpose is only about you and your own family, you don't have a bigger purpose. A bigger purpose would involve multiple people for a set, successful goal. Be persistent about your deterministic creative process rather than the outcome. If the purpose, the creative process, and the goal aligns well, your outcome of success is imminent.

Early Sacrifices for Later Rewards

Society is growing with entrepreneurship-minded people. Make sure your purpose is not just about the money; you should be inclined to create the wealth through various medium, and the money could be an incidental. Learn to limit your entertainment time at the beginning while you have your full-time job and your own business adventures, for much bigger rewards than the early small pleasures. People, who go after the money, either choose the wrong path or they end up in the wrong place, or they get frustrated for the wrong reason. I have invested my time and money for a long time in my real estate projects, in order to harvest later in my life as I wish. I have invested my time and money in small businesses, and I am now focusing on a technology company for bigger success.

I found that intelligently letting the brain and the money work for you, would increase your wealth faster than if you were physically working every day to bring in the money. As you know, the money does not give you the success or the pleasure, but it gives you the power to purchase and help others. These days, it is so easy to get distracted and not be efficient. Social networks and the fast phase of technology are taking society to a different world. Some people are even risking their lives taking selfies in dangerous locations; they post the pictures to get likes or followers on social media. Make sure to sacrifice your momentary pleasures to achieve your long-term enormous success. When I was working full-time, I sacrificed my after-work TV time, and then I gradually even had to quit playing badminton in order to focus on my businesses. My persistent hard work, and the early sacrifices, enabled me to make the big decision, which I will be sharing with you soon.

Don't Forget to Treat Yourself and Spend Time with Your Loved Ones and Friends

I know how hard it is to grow your business vigorously while having a full-time job, and not being able to spend your time with your loved ones and friends. Unfortunately, you only have 24 hours in a day. After doing all these activities, you need enough time to sleep as well. It is a real challenge. I started getting into investments to feel the financial freedom, with my set purpose, when my son was three years old, and my daughter was just one year. At the time, I was working at Blackberry, and I had to travel for company trips while on the weekends I had to travel for my own business purposes. Since I was able to multitask, patiently and professionally, I was able to handle it all at once. Since my kids were toddlers, they also needed lot of my attention at the time. I am very grateful my wife was able to take care of both kids whenever I was out of town, numerous times, for many years. If you start the process earlier than I had started, you will have less stress than what I went through. I am glad I survived and got through it.

I had the good habit of leaving whatever stress or complications I had at work, at the door steps of those companies. I don't carry the emotions, and release my stress at home. Some people would be grumpy at home because they were upset about what has happened at work. That behaviour would damage your happiness and productivity outside of your work. Similar to my own adventurous project issues, I left it at home; and only if I had to make phone calls, or meetings needed to be taken care of for my own business during work hours, I have attended them.

When you take on multiple things, even though your time is limited, make sure to allocate and spend your time with your loved ones. Life is too short, and time cannot be bought back with money. You don't want to get isolated from your friends either. Spend some valuable time and chill out. You have to learn to balance your life from multiple aspects. Since you had been working hard, you should be treated with perks too. Be careful with that. Some people would treat themselves too much, while others would work hard, like being their own slave, and not treat themselves at all. I was supposed to buy a Porsche this year, but I invested all the money into one of my start-up companies. Soon, I will treat myself with something better than what I had planned this year. Let's hope for the best. I am extremely excited for you. Now is the time to learn about how to make the final decision, and break the biweekly prison. Let's learn the feeling of financial independence.

Chapter 14

Fire Your Job and Become Your Own Boss

Once You Start to Feel the Biweekly Prison Break, Confidence Rises

As your independent monthly income rises, while you still have a full-time paying job, your confidence level increases. The capability of handling things becomes easier for you once the confidence level is high. Promote yourself to turn the high energy, which you will get from the confidence, into positive energy. I remember, a couple of years back, when my consulting income was increasing and my net worth was growing silently without me realizing the direct benefit—I felt so good about it. My confidence level increased rapidly, but I never let myself be taken over by it. I still kept my objective of accumulating income properties till the last minute. I will tell you that this is the time when some people may get cocky and buy expensive cars and houses. This kind of premature attitude may intimidate others, and even your business partners. Make sure to treat yourself once you are ready to sustain that lifestyle for a longer period of time, even after you quit your job or encounter any losses in your business.

If you are a professional, or experienced trade, now you have the confidence and the energy. It is now the time you are in a position to negotiate or ask for the things you were afraid of asking for before, at work. You would have been hesitant before, because you would have been afraid of losing your job. Now, if you are in a position where you don't have to worry about anyone else's thoughts, go and ask for things, on your terms. The worst case is if they don't agree, but you can say, "Sure, no problem." In a few months, you are not going to be there anyway. If they agree, you could be their consultant, even for a couple of days per week, while your business takes off.

Whenever you feel that you are lost, or need to refocus, come back and read the book again. Even if you need a mentor in your life to guide you to achieve your purpose, you can reach me at **www.fireyourjobbook.com**. You will be surprised that you are now ready to be free from your day-to-day, regular job. This is the time you may get salary raises, and even other lucrative job opportunities. In my case, I had a salary raise and a bonus waiting for me after a successful project, and I even had a couple of other companies approach me to join them, but I had paved a path to follow my much bigger purpose, and I had to be sincere about it.

Focus On Sales and Business Development

It does not matter what business you are in. You must focus on the proper marketing and sales that would boost your revenue. Many people work hard to develop the actual product they try to sell, but they fail to budget sufficient funds for the marketing. As an entrepreneur, you had better be a good visionary salesperson, for various reasons. You have to attract business partners, investments, employees, and customers. Instead of trying to forcefully sell your passionate product in the market, be creative, and turn your passionate product into someone's problem-solving solution.

When you sell something, make sure it becomes a problem solver for others. For an example, when you rent your income-producing rental property, it is a shelter service you are providing. This is something the entire human race needs to survive. Now, you should know why real estate investment never goes wrong, if you keep it for a long period of time. It is essential for any living thing on this earth. God only made the land once on this earth, and it cannot be reproduced. If you need any training in sales and marketing, you should get yourself trained. If you are not an expert on it, go out and hire the best one.

Now, your business is taking off, and the sale volume is increasing. Make sure your company is growing proportionally. You had better spend money at the appropriate times to treat your existing employees and contractors. If you need to hire more expert contractors, or outsource the job, feel free to do so. Even though I am a real estate investor, and have been doing this for the past 10 years or so, I can't do a plumbing job. I have learned to understand the principles and theory behind it. If a contractor tried to quote me high price, I know enough to negotiate with the trade as per the potential estimated material and the labour cost, but I don't do it myself.

If I had a business model of doing everything myself, I would only own a couple of properties maximum, in the same neighborhood where I live. In my case, I have owned properties in multiple cities with my investment partners. You should focus on developing your business in a professional way, for an exponential growth, as soon as you start to focus on it full-time. You could also hire business development managers to take your business to the next level. Even though you need to know everything, you don't need to know the minor details. Hire the expert, and let them do the work you are supposed to do. As long as they meet or surpass your set goals, your business would move in the right direction.

Leave with a Good Reputation

Now, your months, weeks, or even days are ticking at your workplace. You would even start to feel that you are about to fly. However, don't get emotional and ruin your reputation in a few weeks, which took you many years to build. Make sure to focus on your assigned tasks, and get them finished before you depart. Now, as per your plan, and your own financial comfort, if you decide to break the biweekly prison, set up a time with your manager and break the news. Don't be too optimistic about the lucrative business opportunity you are pursuing. I would recommend you to forget about all the negativity you had within the company. Even though you are tempted, this is not the time to complain about the poor salary raise you had, or the lack of promotions or appreciation by the company. It is time for you to thank the company for giving you the opportunity for you to contribute and grow. The professional experience you were able to accumulate was a catalyst for you to be a better and wiser person today.

Whether you like it or not, this particular company is going to be in your history as the last place you ever worked as an employee. You never know, if there is a financial need, you could do part-time consulting for the current employer. Instead of thinking the current employer is going to be your former employer, treat them as your new reference for the upcoming business references. You may need to tell this news to your colleagues too. Instead of having rumours fill others' heads with your news, it is better that you inform your colleagues, with whom you have shared ideas, office space, numerous collaborative meetings, and company parties about your decision. When you take the time to inform your colleagues about your upcoming departure, they would respect your professionalism. They would feel that you have cared about and respected them.

Now is the best time to hand over your own company business cards to your colleagues and management. If they want to invest, or have an interest in your business to be your customer, they could be in touch with you. Marketing starts now, in your workplace, for your own business. If you would have prematurely distributed your business cards, without knowing the direction of your business, it wouldn't have helped you at all. You should thank your colleagues for being friendly and helpful while you were working along with them. Don't leave any negative feelings, and do not burn your bridges that got you where you are today.

The Day I Fired My Job...

At this stage in your life, your business is growing in a positive direction. You are financially secure enough to embrace the upcoming ups and downs. You are ready to walk out of your job, with good memories. You are ecstatic about your new journey as an independent, one hundred percent, dedicated entrepreneur to your business.

BTW, I want you to be aware I wrote the upcoming contents last year, in the days before I left the company I was working for, and became a butterfly to pursue my ambition. I had a great working relationship with my colleagues and the management, while I really enjoyed the technically challenging projects I had worked on. My discipline and dedication to my entrepreneurship led me to execute the decision, which you want to do some day. It's been over a year now, and I have no regrets; nowadays, I am investing in me, and my businesses, more than ever.

I informed the Syntronic management, right after the completion of the project I was working on, that I would leave the company due to moving with my family to the Greater Toronto Area. My manager had set up a meeting on August 11, 2017, at 1 pm, to sign the departure documents. I had also set up a lunch meet-up with one of my long-term friends. Since I was extremely busy at work in the past, we had been putting off that lunch meet-up. When I met my friend at the restaurant, I told him that I was leaving Ottawa and moving to the Toronto area. I even told him that I was planning to pursue my own business, and handed my business card to him. He started to ask lots of questions about my business I am developing, and the potentials. I was happy to explain it to him, with passion.

When you have passion for something, and have the confidence, your ideas flow automatically. My friend wasn't happy with how engineers and high technology workers in North America would often get laid off. He even had to move around quite a lot, and had to accept a few contract jobs out of town, causing him to be away from his family numerous times. He was so eager to understand more about my own business projects, and showed high interest in participating in one of those projects. It was an awesome, leisurely lunch meeting that turned into a business meeting. We had to cut the lunch meeting a little short due to my other meeting at work, but we agreed to meet again for a business meeting.

I could have worked three more weeks, to the end of my agreed resignation date, but I was paid for those three weeks, and could go as I wished. It was an exceptional day for me to go back to work and collect all my items by myself and leave the company. In the past, I was asked to leave the company through layoffs. This time, I had asked myself to leave the office with confidence.

When I got home, my kids were already home from school. I knew my kids watched me staying up late working on my own projects, while at the same time, coming back from work late, and going to work on the weekends to get things done. As soon as I entered the house, I broke the news that I was no longer an employee for anyone, and from now on, I was going to be my own boss, and take on my passion. My nine-year-old daughter ran towards me, and hugged and congratulated me. I was so surprised by her action, then she told me, "Dad, I am glad that you can now spend your time on your own business, and spend more time with us, instead of trying to juggle your full-time work, your own business, and trying to spend time with us." At that moment, my confidence and my energy level sky rocketed, along with my responsibility to make my own business endeavours more successful than ever.

I would encourage you to be truthful. Never abandon your promises; be passionate about what you want to do; and be hungry to learn more, and develop your business with confidence. Business partners, and the employees, want to deal with a confident entrepreneur, with the leadership skills and right attitude. A biweekly prison break is not a one-day thing—it takes time, sacrifices, courage, the right attitude and determination. Don't have regrets later in your life by not pursuing your passion. The majority of people think they are saving by clinging onto little things, but they don't realize the abundance of opportunities they are losing. Your success can be only controlled by you. Get out of your comfort zone, and do something useful for yourself and your future generation.

About the Author

Akilan Aks Theva was born in Jaffna, Sri Lanka, and started his early businesses at the age of 13. He moved to Canada when he was 17 years of age, due to civil war. With his tireless, hardworking, and deterministic attitude, he became a successful Radio Frequency (RF) Design Engineer, and worked in the high-tech industry for 20 years.

Due to his frustration of getting laid off and not having control of his own investment, he started to invest in real estate. He is a credible and knowledgeable real estate investor and an entrepreneur.

At the age of 42, Akilan decided to pursue independence from the biweekly prison, and became a full-time real estate investor and entrepreneur. He founded a company, called BisRing (www.bisring.com): a real estate marketing company for all kinds of real estate users and marketers.

Akilan is a great person to do business with and learn from. He lives in Richmond Hill, Canada, with his wife and two kids. His updates and contact information can be found at **www.fireyourjobbook.com**.